D0731488

Contemporary Studies in Literature

Eugene Ehrlich, *Columbia University*
Daniel Murphy, *City University of New York*
Series Editors

Volumes include:

Samuel Beckett

a collection of criticism edited by Ruby Cohn

McGraw-Hill Book Company

New York • St. Louis • San Francisco • Auckland • Düsseldorf • Johannesburg
Kuala Lumpur • London • Mexico • Montreal • New Delhi • Panama • Paris
São Paulo • Singapore • Sydney • Tokyo • Toronto

Excerpts from the works of Samuel Beckett are reprinted in this volume by permission of Grove Press, Inc., New York, Faber and Faber, Ltd., London, and Calder and Boyars, Ltd., London.

Chronology of Beckett's Life and Chronology of Beckett's Work, from *Back to Beckett* by Ruby Cohn, pp. vii–xii, xiii–xv (Copyright © 1973 by Princeton University Press), reprinted by permission of Princeton University Press.

123456789MUMU798765

Library of Congress Cataloging in Publication Data

Cohn, Ruby, comp.

Main entry under title:

Samuel Beckett: a collection of criticism

  (Contemporary studies in literature) (McGraw-Hill paperbacks)

  Bibliography: p.
  1. Beckett, Samuel, 1906– —Criticism and interpretation—Addresses, essays, lectures. I. Abbot, H. Porter. II. Cohn, Ruby.
PR6003.E282Z815   848'.9'1409   75-8673

ISBN 0-07-011598-2

Contents

Chronology of Beckett's Life

1906   April 13 (Good Friday), Samuel Barclay Beckett was born in Foxrock, near Dublin, Ireland. "I have a clear memory of my own fetal existence. It was an existence where no voice, no possible movement could free me from the agony and darkness I was subject to." (Gruen) He was the second and last son of Mary and William Beckett.

1910   Earliest extant photograph of Beckett was the result of the photographer's need of a subject for the title, "Bedtime." Beckett was posed praying at his mother's knee. "[I was brought up] almost a Quaker. But I soon lost faith. I don't think I ever had it after leaving Trinity." (Hobson)

1911   He attended kindergarten named Miss Ida Elsner's Academy. "You might say I had a happy childhood . . . although I had little talent for happiness. My parents did everything that could make a child happy. But I was often lonely." (Harvey)

1912   He attended Earlsfort House School in Dublin, where he began to study French and piano.

1920   He attended Portora Royal School in Northern Enniskillen, where his brother Frank had preceded him. The school emphasized sports, and Samuel Beckett was on the cricket and rugby teams. He excelled also at tennis, swimming, and boxing. He began to write poems and stories, some of which were published in the school newspaper.

1923   He attended Trinity College, Dublin, living at home in Foxrock. His school sports were limited to cricket and golf as he became more absorbed in the academic curriculum.

1925   He studied Dante.

1926   He spent his summer vacation bicycling through the Loire Valley.

1927   He spent his summer vacation in Florence.
In December he took his B.A. degree.

1928   He spent the spring term as French tutor in Campbell College, Belfast.
In October, he took up a two-year fellowship at l'École Normale Supérieure in Paris. There he was befriended by Joyce. He did research on the life and works of Descartes.

1929   He published fiction and criticism in *transition*. He participated in the twenty-fifth Bloomsday celebration, but he had to be "ingloriously abandoned . . . in one of those temporary palaces which are inseparably associated with the memory of the Emperor Vespasian." (Ellmann)

1930   He won first prize for a poem on Time, in a contest sponsored by Nancy Cunard, who later wrote of *Whoroscope*: "This long poem, mysterious, obscure in parts, centered around Descartes, was clearly by someone intellectual and highly educated."

With Alfred Péron, he translated into French the "Anna Livia Plurabelle" section of Joyce's *Work in Progress*. He spent the summer vacation writing a study of Proust, with the intention of pursuing his academic career. In September, he returned to Trinity as Assistant in French. "Sam would stand for minutes staring through the window and then throw a perfectly constructed sentence to his crumb-picking avid audience." (Leventhal) Beckett read the *Ethics* of Arnold Geulincx.

1931   In February, with Georges Pelorson, he wrote *Le Kid*, a parody of Corneille's *Cid*, and he played Don Diègue. The Trinity College newspaper lampooned him: "An exhausted aesthete who all life's strange poisonous wines has sipped, and found them rather tedious." Also: "I wish he would explain his explanations." He made friends with Jack Yeats. In December he took his M.A. degree.

1932   Fleeing to the Continent, Beckett celebrated the new year by resigning from Trinity. "He could not bear the absurdity of teaching to others what he did not know himself." (Coe) "The College wits murmured that he wrote his resignation on a scroll of bumph but those in authority wailed because with him went the College master key." (Leventhal) He traveled in Germany and returned to Paris in March, beginning work on *Dream of Fair to Middling Women*. He translated Surrealist poems into English. Lucia Joyce was infatuated with him. After the assassination of French President Paul Doumer, he returned to Foxrock because his papers were not in order.

1933   In June, William Beckett died of a heart attack. "What am I to do now but follow his trace over the fields and hedges." (Harvey) Beckett's brother Frank succeeded their father in the surveying firm of Beckett and Metcalfe. Beckett received an annuity of two hundred pounds a year, and he exiled himself to London, where he spent nearly three years—"bad in every way, financially, psychologically." (Fletcher) Later, Beckett noted: "They always know you're an Irishman. The porter in the hotel. His tone changes. The taxi-man says, 'Another sixpence, Pat.' They call you Pat.'' (Sigal)

1934 He published *More Pricks Than Kicks* and began *Murphy*.

1936–37 He visited museums in Germany, uneasy at Nazi oppression of Jewish intellectuals.

1937 In the fall, he returned to Paris and renewed his friendship with Joyce, also making friends among painters. He wrote his first poems in French. In November, he returned to Dublin as a witness in an antisemitic defamation trial against Oliver St. John Gogarty: "It is soon established that the witness himself is author of a banned book (the title was enough; no censor would risk his immortal soul by reading it) called *More Pricks Than Kicks*. Counsel dare not speak its name. The Dublin evening papers carried banner headlines: THE ATHEIST FROM PARIS.'' (Leventhal) Living at Foxrock during the trial and afterward, Beckett wrote a friend: "I have done little work, that little on the Great Cham, in the hopes of making a play of his relations with Mrs. Thrale.''

1938 On January 7, walking along a Paris street, Beckett was stabbed by a stranger. Joyce described the injury in a letter to his son: "The stab was above the heart; that is uninjured, and the lungs also, but there is a perforation of the pleura, the layer of tissue surrounding the lungs. My house on the day after your departure was like the stock exchange, telephone calls from everywhere. . . . Beckett has had a lucky escape.'' In the hospital, Beckett was visited by pianist Suzanne Dumesnil, who later became his wife. Once well, Beckett asked his imprisoned assailant why he had attacked him. "Je ne sais pas, monsieur,'' was the answer. In fall, Beckett found a small apartment at 6, rue des Favorites, near the slaughterhouses and the Impasse de l'Enfant-Jésus, which was his home until 1961. With the help of Alfred Péron, he began to translate *Murphy* into French. Beckett has described 1938–39 as "a period of apathy and lethargy.''

1939 In September, war broke out while he was visiting his mother in Ireland. He returned at once to Paris. "I preferred France in war to Ireland in peace.'' (Shenker)

1940 In June, Beckett fled Paris. In Vichy, he saw Joyce, who arranged for Valéry Larbaud to cash his Irish check, enabling Beckett to go as far South as Toulouse. In October, he returned to occupied Paris. Through Alfred Péron, he joined a Resistance network. "I couldn't stand with my arms folded.'' (Reid)

Thirty of the eighty members of his network survived World War II.

1942   Beckett escaped hours before the Nazis searched his apartment, having been warned by a wire from Madame Péron: "Alfred arrêté par Gestapo. Prière faire nécessaire pour corriger l'erreur." The "nécessaire" was to obtain false papers and flee to Free France, stopping at Roussillon in the Vaucluse. For two years Beckett spent his days doing agricultural work and his nights writing *Watt*.

1945   On May 8, Armistice. Beckett went to Ireland to visit his mother and brother. Finding it difficult to return to France, he joined an Irish Red Cross unit that left for war-ravaged Saint-Lô in August. There he served as interpreter and storekeeper for a field hospital. By winter he was back in his Paris apartment.

1946   He began five years of writing in French—his most fertile period. "I wrote all my work very fast—between 1946 and 1950. Since then I haven't written anything. Or at least nothing that has seemed to me valid." (Shenker)

1950   He returned to Ireland in time to see his mother die.

1953   On January 5, première of *En attendant Godot* at Théâtre de Babylone, Paris.

1954   He returned to Ireland in time to see his brother die.

1958   In February, the English Lord Chancellor refused to allow production of *Endgame* in London, since the Deity was called a bastard. The ban was lifted in November.
       In February, the Dublin Drama Festival Committee dropped O'Casey's *Drums of Father Ned*, whereupon Beckett refused permission for any of his works to be produced in Ireland. Permission was regranted as of May 1960.

1959   He received an honorary doctorate from his Alma Mater, Trinity College.

1961   He shared the International Publishers' Prize with Jorge Luis Borges.

1964   He visited New York City to take part in the filming of his *Film*.

1966   He directed the first French production of *Va et Vient*, his first independent direction. He then directed a German television version of his *Eh Joe*.

1967   He directed a German stage version of his *Endgame*.

1969   He directed a German stage version of his *Krapp's Last Tape*.

1970	While vacationing in Tunisia, he was awarded the Nobel Prize in Literature. Earlier, he directed French stage versions of *Krapp's Last Tape* and *Acts Without Words 1* and *2*.
1971	He directed a German stage version of his *Happy Days*.
1975	He directed a German stage version of his *Waiting for Godot*.

Sources of Quotations

Coe, Richard N. *Samuel Beckett* (New York, 1964).

Cunard, Nancy. *These Were the Hours* (Carbondale, Ind., 1969).

Ellmann, Richard. *James Joyce* (New York, 1959).

Fletcher, John. *The Novels of Samuel Beckett* (London, 1964).

Gruen, John. "Samuel Beckett Talks About Beckett," *Vogue* (December, 1969).

Harvey, Lawrence. *Samuel Beckett, Poet and Critic* (Princeton, N.J., 1970).

Hobson, Harold. "Samuel Beckett, Dramatist of the Year," *International Theatre Annual* (London, 1956).

Leventhal, A. J. in *Beckett at Sixty* (London, 1967).

Reid, Alec. *All I Can Manage, More Than I Could* (Dublin, 1968).

Shenker, Israel. "Moody Man of Letters," *New York Times* (May 6, 1956).

Sigal, Clancy. "Is This the Person to Murder Me?" *Sunday Times* (March 1, 1964).

Chronology of Beckett's Work

Year*	Poetry	Fiction	Drama	Criticism
1929		Assumption Che Sciagura		Dante . . . Bruno Vico . . Joyce
1930	Whoroscope From the only Poet . . . For Future Reference			
1931	Return to the Vestry Yoke of Liberty Enueg I, II, Alba Casket of Pralinen . . .		Le Kid	Proust The Possessed
1932	Dortmunder Home Olga	Dream of Fair to Middling Women Dante and the Lobster		
1934	Gnome Malacoda	More Pricks Than Kicks A Case in a Thousand		Leishman Review MacGreevy Review
1935	Echo's Bones Cascando			
1936		Murphy		Jack Yeats Review

*Dates are those of completion, up to the end of 1974.
Titles are given in language originally written. Beckett's translations are noted in parentheses, collections are underlined.

Chronology of Beckett's Work

Year	Poetry	Fiction	Drama	Criticism
1938	Ooftish			Denis Devlin Review
1939	Poèmes			
1944		Watt		
1945	Saint-Lô			
1946	Mort d'A.D.	La Fin (The End–1954)		Review of MacGreevy book on Jack Yeats
		Le Voyage de Mercier et Camier autour du Pot dans les Bosquets de Bondy (Mercier and Camier–1974)		
		Premier Amour (First Love–1972)		La Peinture des van Velde
		Le Calmant (The Calmative–1967)		
		L'Expulsé (The Expelled–1962)		
1947		Molloy (English 1951)	Eleuthéria	
1948	Six Poèmes (Four translated–1961)	Malone meurt (Malone Dies–1956)	En attendant Godot (Waiting for Godot–1954)	Peintres de l'empêchement

Chronology of Beckett's Work

Year	Poetry	Fiction	Drama	Criticism
1963			Cascando Esquisse radiophonique	
1964			Film	
1965		Imagination morte imaginez (Imagination Dead Imagine—1967)	Come and Go	
1966		Assez (Enough—1967) Le Dépeupleur (The Lost Ones—1972) Bing (Ping—1967)	Eh Joe Breath	
1969		Sans (Lessness—1970)		
1971		Work in Regress		
1972		Foirades	Not I	
1974			That Time	

xvi

Though unpublished works are included, this listing is not complete. Beckett is slowly exhuming his unpublished pieces that date mainly from the 1950s and 1960s.

Ruby Cohn

Inexhaustible Beckett: An Introduction

As man and writer, Samuel Beckett believes in his ignorance, impotence, and incoherence. His critics, in contrast, agree that his work forms a rare whole, and yet they disagree on the nature of the wholeness. Even book titles point to divergent interpretations: Niklaus Gessner's *Inadequacy of Language,* Ihab Hassan's *Literature of Silence,* Hugh Kenner's *Stoic Comedians,* Patrick Murray's *Tragic Comedian,* Raymond Federman's *Journey to Chaos,* David Hesla's *Shape of Chaos,* Colin Duckworth's *Angels of Darkness,* Frederick Hoffman's *Language of Self,* Michael Robinson's *Long Sonata of the Dead,* Hans-Joachim Schulz's *Hell of Stories.* We can learn about Beckett from these titles, as from other books simply entitled *Samuel Beckett,* which tell of the art of failure, time's erosion of life, the inadequacy and even impossibility of love, the need of a witness to lend credence to identity, the bankruptcy of a cultural tradition, the encroachment of nothingness on being, the retrieving of personal history from fictional stories. More consistent than any of these themes, perhaps, is Beckett's relentless denudation from work to work, stripping away events, people, objects, motions, emotions, and even words, until a vestigial verbal skeleton complains of its articulation.

Beckett may dwell on several themes, but he dwells in experiential depths probed through a language without which such depths are unfathomable. Through two languages, for Beckett wrote most of his work in French before translating it into English. Beckett's language mastery reaches toward a mystery impervious to language—human essence or elemental being—but the reaching assumes diverse and dazzling forms.

Beginning, as most of us do, with his native language, Beckett turned to French (for sustained work) when he was nearly forty, and

1

French first—with the story paradoxically entitled *The End*—captures his distinctive mode. The typical Beckett tale is told by a narrator passionately observing capricious minutiae while protesting his indifference to them. Then compassion bleeds through the passion, artistry through the apparent anarchy. And through the cold black print sounds what was rare in French fiction of 1946—the vivid rhythm of a speaking voice. Consistent in Beckett's French—from *La Fin* to *Pas Moi*—is a vigorous vulgarity that relates his people to proverbial down-and-outs. Their speech is free of grammatical faults; in spite of occasional anglicisms and the remains—the very threadbare remains—of formal schooling, they revel in popular locutions. Appreciation of Beckett's French is absent from this volume intended for the English-language reader, but that French is nevertheless a matchless achievement. In one of his rare interviews Beckett commented on writing in French, especially the trilogy of novels: "Oh! oui, très difficilement! Mais avec élan, dans une sorte d'enthousiasme."

In praising Beckett's French, we plunge *in medias res*, mid-career, for the early works are of course in English. Other than school juvenilia which are only now being exhumed, Beckett broke into print in 1929 with a piece on *Finnegans Wake* written at the request of James Joyce, an erudite comic dialogue on contraception in Ireland, and a curious short story, "Assumption." Supercilious mannerism marks and mars the three pieces, but already we see generic variety. And from 1929 to 1974 no year has passed without Beckett's pen scribbling or stumbling through the exercise books to which he commits his first drafts. Forty-five years of creative activity, however his characters espouse indolence.

Beckett's early works are more or less minor—less minor as he approaches the French summit (variously located in the trilogy, *Godot, Endgame,* and *How It Is*). Several critics have traced the difficult trail toward the summit, and Beckett himself saw and sometimes drew connections between his separate works. James Joyce suggested the subject of Beckett's essay on *Finnegans Wake* because he knew that the young Trinity College student was deep in Dante, and Dante reappears sporadically until the 1966 *Dépeupleur*. Not only Dante's phrases, but his scenes and characters. After Dante, Descartes. Beckett's first separately published work *Whoroscope*, is a dramatic monologue spoken by René Descartes, who was to gnaw at Beckett for many years. Beckett's Proust study of 1931 is usually viewed as an introduction to Beckett's own fiction. The young Irishman draws irreverently upon the Bible for the title of his first full-length book, *More Pricks Than Kicks*, and biblical shards pierce many subsequent works, especially the plays. But literature is not the only binding thread between Beckett works. He cross-references the separate stories of *More Pricks Than Kicks* with ostentatious footnotes. The Dantean name Mulucoda and an invented name Albu appear both in the stories of *More Pricks* and in the poems of *Echo's Bones*, as do bicycle trips through the Irish countryside. The aloof and unnamed persona of the poems resembles the Dantean-named Belacqua of the stories in that both mock death by mocking life. But in spite of a few shared scenes, people, and attitudes, verse and prose might have different authors; cryptic verse lines condemn the cruelty of living, but polished prose sentences condemn the cruelties of people. In spite of proper names and places, the verse guards a private world; though the prose stories occasionally draw upon Beckett's experience, they parody literature rather than life; they rarely intrude upon the inner self of the protagonist.

Of his early work in three genres—verse, short fiction, criticism—no one could have a lower opinion than Beckett. Reluctant to reprint these pieces, he shies away from remembering them.

The first offspring Beckett acknowledges in his work is *Murphy*, completed as he was turning thirty. The novel looks like a new beginning: no carry-over characters, landscapes, or scenes. Belacqua is Dantean in "his embryonal repose," a far cry from Beckett's compulsive wanderer of the same name in *More Pricks Than Kicks*. But Murphy resembles Belacqua in a susceptibility to jokes. Murphy occasionally sneers in the Belacqua manner, but the novel hero is explicitly designated as "not a puppet."

In sympathy for his protagonist, as well as in conflict, coherence, and clear chronology, *Murphy* embodies Beckett's only concession to the traditional novel. An omniscient narrator tells the story of the protagonist, Murphy, who lives in London (or its outskirts) in 1935, the year the novel was written. Murphy seeks inner peace, but other characters seek Murphy. Chapters on a Keystone Kop triumvirate alternate with chapters about an inward-looking Irishman. Dylan Thomas' review penetrated the sparkling surface: "[*Murphy*] is serious because it is, mainly, the study of a complex and oddly tragic character who cannot reconcile the unreality of the seen world with the reality of the unseen, and who, through scorn and neglect of 'normal' society, drifts into the society of the certified abnormal in his search for 'a little world.'" The sentence aptly describes Beckett's next—and decidedly untraditional—novel *Watt*. And, with the important excision of the word "certified," it is relevant, too, to Beckett's French fiction, where Beckett etches incisive differences in "the reality of the unseen," while the seen recedes toward a vanishing point.

Of all Beckett's heroes, only Murphy assigns specific location to the unseen—the three zones of his mind. Of all Beckett's heroes, only Murphy is an object of desire in the seen world. And Murphy alone finds refuge from normal society in the abnormal. His affections shift from the redundantly and ironically named Celia Kelly, the whore (Latin *caelum*—"sky"), to the accurately named Mr. Endon, the schizophrenic (Greek ενδον—"within"). Like his predecessor Belacqua, Murphy dies by accident; but cool, guarded Belacqua is overanesthetized, whereas ardent Murphy burns to death. Belacqua's widow marries his best friend, but Celia Kelly finally earns her name, achieving a celestial dignity.

Watt is a less finished but more important novel because it signals Beckett's artistic self-discovery. Watt is the first Beckett protagonist to convey the full force of human solitude and the full weakness of human endeavor. Watt is attracted and rejected by an inscrutable Mr. Knott. Journeying toward the reality of the unseen, Watt leaves the unreality of the seen world, confined by Beckett to brief, bright chapters at the beginning and end of the novel. In *Watt*, reality is not so much unseen as impenetrable, for events on Mr. Knott's premises prove to be "of great formal brilliance and indeterminable purport." Yet Watt stubbornly tries to determine their purport. He fails. His process of failing is communicated and imitated through the most problematical prose in all of fiction. A third of Beckett's novel pounds at us with catalogues, alternatives, genealogies, permutations, combinations, logical impossibilities couched in maddening symmetries, and an academic investigation to curdle the conscience of all academics. But in spite of Watt's honest, humorless attempts to use his mind, "of the nature of Mr. Knott himself Watt remained in particular ignorance." As Watt replaced Erskine who replaced Arsene, Watt is replaced by Arthur who will be replaced by Micks. In an infinite series, Mr. Knott's short, chubby servants replace his tall, thin servants (with some discrepancies). But none of them learn anything about their master, who is both steadfast and changing.

Watt spins the yarn of his failure some time after his service period. Sheltered in a pavilion, Watt tells an achronological tale to his neighbor Sam, and Sam tells it to us, or rather, writes it for us. Sam claims to be a scrupulous scribe: "For all I know on the subject of Mr. Knott, and of all that touched Mr. Knott, and on the subject of Watt, and of all that touched Watt, came from Watt, and from Watt alone." But Sam makes this claim as a prelude to possibilities of error in Watt's yarn. And indeed Beckett's yarn about a hero of meticulous exactitude is itself riddled with errors of calculation, incomplete lists, and falsification of phrasing ("a little fat bottom sticking out in front and a little fat belly sticking out behind"). Into his prose of exhaustive enumeration Beckett has inserted flaws, and other flaws have entered inadvertently into this book about a man whose mind is schooled to flawless reason.

Beckett's next hero—nameless—will know better. Watt, a would-be Cartesian, thinks in order to try to be, but his nameless successor, adopting the language of Descartes, will deliberately *not* think in order to be. He will let the stream of sentences carry him where they will—up to The End that gives Beckett's first French story its name. About half the story appeared in *Les Temps Modernes* (July, 1946), as "Suite," but there was no *suite*, and a notebook at the University of Texas library contains Beckett's draft of an indignant letter to Simone de Beauvoir. *The End* did not appear in its entirety until 1955, when it was included as one of the stories in *Stories* and *Texts for Nothing*. Of the four stories Beckett wrote in 1946, he discarded *First Love* (until 1970) and he ordered the other three into what he has called "Prime," "Death," and "Limbo." But before he penned "Prime" and "Death" (*The Expelled* and *The Calmative*), he wrote his first French novel, *Mercier et Camier*, finally translated into English in 1974.

Like English *Watt*, French *Mercier et Camier* was considered by its author as an exercise, an experiment. But even in experiment, there is sureness of grasp. Beckett revised *Watt* several times during a four-year period in which he fled from his Paris apartment to a Roussillon farmhouse. Back in Paris, with World War II finally over, Beckett wrote with prolific zest, producing four long stories, four novels, and two plays—in French. In contrast to the four year's work on *Watt*, *Mercier et Camier* was completed in less than three months (July to September, 1946), and the manuscript shows only minor changes. Yet Beckett was so dissatisfied with it that he did not permit its publication until 1970.

As the title indicates, the protagonist is a couple. The original title, confined to the manuscript, is more revealing. *Le Voyage de Mercier et Camier autour du Pot dans les Bosquets de Bondy* might be translated as *The Perpetual Detours of Mercier and Camier in a Den of Thieves*. In Beckett's first French novel, Mercier and Camier meet to take this journey of perpetual detours from an indeterminate destination. Their human encounters might be viewed as biblical thieves. Older and perhaps wiser than Watt, Mercier and Camier confine their questions and observations to the immediate practicalities of their journey:

> We're progressing painfully—
> Painfully! Mercier burst forth.
> Arduously, arduously through somber and relatively abandoned streets, probably because of the late hour and uncertain weather, not knowing who is leading nor who following. [my translation]

On their voyage they meet several people, among them characters from *Watt* and *The End*. Their last encounter is with Watt himself, who refers to Murphy and who reunites Mercier and Camier after their temporary separation. But when Watt arouses the fury of bar companions by cursing at life, they abandon him. Mercier and Camier walk a short way together and then separate at evening: "In the dark [Mercier] also heard better, he heard sounds that the long day had hidden from him, human murmurs for example, and the rain on the water."

During the course of the novel, bright conversational duets alternate with lyrical passages that might be landscape or soulscape, describing the damp fall of night. After *Mercier et Camier* Beckett committed the conversational verve to another genre, drama. Soulscape became the shifting ground of his further fiction.

Soulscape ostensibly painted by a narrating "I." But the identity of the "I"changes in the stories, in the novels, in the *Texts for Nothing*, and in the fragments of *How It Is*. Each "I" composes his own world —physical and metaphysical. Beckett may not be a "myriad-minded" Shakespeare, but there is vivid diversity in his individual works, which have been too easily grouped as repetitious. They are repetitious, to be sure, of image, phrase, even scene; of comic glimmers in a tragic night. But each work is a fresh attack on silence, launched by a highly individualized attacker.

In each of the Stories, a nameless man rambles through events in his past. These men live on the outskirts of society, but they have memories of their fathers, whom they associate with hats and bequests of money. Old and sorely afflicted, they seize on inventive means of survival: one spends a day in a horse-drawn carriage, the next kisses a stranger in return for a phial of calmatives, the last milks a resisting cow into his hat. Common to all the Stories is the juxtaposition of traveling against shelter. And common to all the Stories is the overriding fact that they are stories.

The Stories reveal Beckett building a new, seemingly makeshift structure with his new language. Conflict, climax, and dénouement are absent from these alogical cumulations of events. Hesitation, self-correction, lapses into the present tense endow the first French tales with an oral quality that is not quite captured in the English versions. And yet that oral quality is subtly undermined by a syntactical variety rare in everyday speech. Most faithful to common speech are sudden eruptions of feeling, which stamp the narration more clearly than its subject matter. Each of the narrators indicates that subject matter is arbitrary:

The Expelled   "No reason for this to end or go on. Then let it end."
The Calmative "I'll tell my story in the past none the less, as
            though it were a myth, or an old fable, for this evening I need another

age, that age to become another age in which I became what I was.''
The End ''The memory came faint and cold of the story I might have
told, a story in the likeness of my life, I mean without the
courage to end or the strength to go on.''

These feeble but febrile narrators deceive our expectations about
stories: plot fragments into incidents, character into a nameless mercurial
''I,'' places into a static montage. The Stories challenge our reading
habits, forcing us to linger over each sentence, to absorb form as well as
information.

The reach toward formal immediacy and condensation is the legacy
of the Story heroes to the novel heroes, Molloy, Moran, Malone, and the
Unnamable. Four narrator-heroes in three books which Beckett refers to
as a trilogy. But rather than trace the adventures of the same hero from
book to book, Beckett traces the adventures of differently named heroes.
Like the Stories, the novels might be entitled ''Prime,'' ''Death,'' and
''Limbo.'' In the first novel, Molloy and Moran deteriorate physically,
but their narrations acquire power so that they achieve a creative *prime*.
Malone Dies is the apt title of a fiction grounded on the process of *dying*.
The Unnamable lives in *limbo*. And even more obsessively than the Story
heroes, the novel heroes tell tales. Molloy seeks his mother, and Moran
seeks Molloy; both write an account of a fruitless search. Malone writes
so as to fill (and fulfill?) the time of his dying. And the Unnamable
disowns the written for the spoken word, whosever the voice that may
speak it.

These writings, the novels we read, undermine the reality of their
and our visible world, so as to suggest the reality of an invisible, interior
life. In the undermining process lies an overpowering impression of
individual authenticity. Though they share many attributes, bourgeois
Moran is not to be confused with tramp Molloy. And both are distin-
guishable from moribund Malone. The Unnamable is undescribable; yet
he diverges from Moran, Molloy, or Malone. On the other hand, they
resemble one another. Many circumstantial details link Moran to Molloy,
and failing senses link Malone to both of them. But each narrator builds
with words a world to his dimensions.

Molloy opens his novel with simple declarative sentences which are
soon riddled with ''perhaps.'' The tenth short sentence introduces us to
writing: ''He gives me money and takes away the pages.'' In spite of
pages, however, Molloy's writing is even more oral than that of the Story
protagonists; contractions (''It wasn't true love.''), questions (''For what
then?''), corrections (''It was he told me I'd begun all wrong, that I
should have begun differently.'') in the very first paragraph contribute to
Molloy's immediacy. As Moran will say of him: ''His whole body was a

vociferation.'' And his vociferations engrave scenes in our memory—the meeting of A and C, Molloy's communication with his mother through blows on the head, the funeral of Lousse's dog, memories of an urchin's thanks for picking up his marble and of romance in a rubbish dump, the elegance with which Molloy sacrifices the principle of trim in the distribution of his sucking-stones, and the way he feels at peace at the bottom of a ditch.

Moran begins in even simpler, more declarative sentences, but they announce his doom. Moran's cruelties to his son reflect Molloy's cruelties to his mother, but all tenderness is spent. Though both recorders belong to a Kafkaesque organization, Molloy towers above it whereas Moran fits snugly into it. He follows habit in following its orders: ''Next I attacked, according to my custom, the capital question of the effects to take with me.'' The d's, t's, and k's echo his machine-gun mind. Moran's early scenes succeed each other swiftly, springing from realistic small town life—his son's enema, his dishonest communion, his servant's solitude. Once Moran begins to think about Molloy, however, he thinks like Molloy. And the scenes of his voyage are as disturbing as those involving Molloy—giving bread to a man with a stick, bashing in the skull of his double, lying on his stomach to look for his dispersed keys, confronting Gaber in the middle of a forest, recollecting the dance of his bees.

Near the end of their quests Molloy and Moran refer to themselves by name, and the references show the import of their journeys:

> Molloy could stay, where he happened to be.
> [The voice] did not use the words that Moran had been taught when he was little and that he in turn had taught to his little one.

Moran has had to unlearn the language of the seen world in order to set out (on crutches) and set forth (in writing) toward a mythic reality which was Molloy's starting point. Molloy has learned to subdue his will, to accept both being and nothingness—and to record the process of arriving at acceptance.

Of the four narrators of the trilogy, Malone is most endearingly situated in his here and now. We know little of the rooms of Molloy and Moran, but we know Malone's room well—his bed, cupboard, small table on wheels which he reaches with his hooked stick so as to avail himself of the pot of soup or the pot for slops. We even know several treasures in his cupboard—one boot, three socks, a pipe bowl, a packet wrapped in newspaper, a needle between two corks, a photograph of an ass, the top of a crutch, the cap of a bicycle bell, a bloody club

—reminiscent of scenes in the fiction that precedes his account. But above all we know Malone himself, hirsute under his hat, naked under his bedclothes, almost paralyzed except for frantic fingers pushing a stub of pencil across the pages of his exercise book.

Unlike Molloy and Moran, Malone is under no orders to write, nor, Belacqua-like, to relive his past. He plants himself determinedly in his moribund present. What he will commit to his notebook is a description of that present, an inventory of his possessions, and his stories. He wavers between four stories—of man, woman, thing, and animal—and three; with "the man and the woman in the same story, there is so little difference between a man and a woman, between mine I mean." But when his fictional Sapo grows into Macmann, confined to an asylum, Malone immerses us in a love story—*Vive la différence!* Macmann and his Moll do their geriatric utmost to fan the difference into a flicker of passion. Though the dying storyteller kills Moll off, Macmann lasts almost as long as Malone, who dies into the deaths of his characters, having earlier lived himself in their lives.

The asylum attendant Lemuel goes berserk and hacks away at his charges, after which Malone hacks away at his prose:

> Lemuel is in charge, he raises his hatchet on which the blood will never dry, but not to hit anyone, he will not hit anyone, he will not hit anyone any more, he will not touch anyone any more, with it or with it or with it or with or
> > or with it or with his hammer or with his stick or with his fist or in thought in dream I mean never he will never
> > or with his pencil or with his stick or
> > or light light I mean
> > never there he will never
> > never anything
> > there
> > any more

In its interruptive simplicity, the passage seems agonizingly faithful to mortality. And by the end of *Malone Dies*, fussy, programmatic Malone emerges as a mythic giant who "would fill a considerable part of the universe."

"My story ended I'll be living yet," Malone has threatened, so he reapppears to the Unnamable. But the Unnamable speaks without appearing at all. All Beckett's French heroes might twist the *cogito* to "I suffer therefore I am," but the Unnamable, who suffers most, can draw from suffering no certainty of being; he suffers most because he can draw no certainties. (And Beckett himself found *The Unnamable* so painful to write that he digressed with *Waiting for Godot* between the second and third volumes of the trilogy.)

Molloy, the first volume of the trilogy, contains two deliberately contrasting stories—Molloy's and Moran's—to arrive at a suggestion of convergence. The second and third volumes of the trilogy contrast without converging. Malone expires in the spirit of method, whereas the Unnamable exudes lack of method. Malone tries to note a detailed inventory of his surroundings, whereas the Unnamable is totally divorced from empirical reality. Malone hopes to record the process of dying, whereas the Unnamable is not sure he is alive. Malone tells stories from which he vigilantly tries to exclude himself, whereas the Unnamable cannot sustain the preposterous tales in which he cannot find himself. Malone despairs of the power of stories, whereas the Unnamable affirms the impotence of words but is unable to divest himself of them.

The Unnamable is hard to read and hard to discuss. Time and place, coordinates of reality, vanish, so that only two scenes can be visualized—both from stories: crippled Mahood returns to his family-filled rotunda, and legless Mahood broods in his jar outside a restaurant and opposite a slaughter house. Worm is created to be without story or attributes, and so he is. Most of *The Unnamable* circles about an unidentifiable near abstraction who nevertheless weaves arabesques of anguish with negatives, interrogatives, antecedentless pronouns, and a rush of phrases that prevent sentences from coming to completion.

Beckett's trilogy is told by four different narrators who are at once the same and touchingly different. They subsume Beckett's earlier characters. Moran—"What a rabble in my head, what a gallery of moribunds. Murphy, Watt, Yerk, Mercier and all the others." Malone—"Then it will be all over with the Murphys, Merciers, Molloys, Morans and Malones, unless it goes on beyond the grave." And the Unnamable thrice refers to the protagonists who precede him—"but their day is done." Each narrator devours his predecessor, but as Belacqua had affinities with the persona of the poems, so—and more strongly—the fictional heroes from Murphy to Malone show a family resemblance, which also includes the Unnamable in certain lights. Mainly the light by which experience is objectified and comprehended through narrative. After *The Unnamable*, stories are abortive in Beckett's prose; like dialogue, they surface in his drama.

Beckett has stated that drama is relaxation for him: "You have a definite space and people in this space. That's relaxing." Of that relaxation Beckett has built his best-known works—seven stage plays, four radio plays, two mime plays, a film, and a television play. (I list only those that have been produced.) The concealed variety of the fiction bursts forth from the dramatic genres, as from each play within these genres. No living author in English or French has molded his words so skillfully into both fiction and drama, while paradoxically and despairingly protesting his own failure.

Two frayed comedians by a tree, a throned figure and two ashbins, an aging blonde half buried under a hellish light, a wearish old man bent over a tape recorder, three greyish faces atop three grey urns, three almost faceless women, changing light on a cluttered stage, a mouth adrift in the dark—these are Beckett's theater images, at once specific and metaphoric. His stage space is excruciatingly definite, and so are his people. The late Jack MacGowran has spoken of the range and challenge of Beckett's roles, having played Lucky in *Godot,* Tommy in *All That Fall*, Clov in *Endgame*, the actor-victim of *Act Without Words 1,* Henry in *Embers,* the face in *Eh Joe,* and the several characters in his anthology *Beginning to End*. Roger Blin, who has played and directed several Beckett plays, remarked that one had to be in top form to enact Beckett's mutilated people. It is form—daring individuation of form—that relates Beckett's fiction to his drama. And as in the fiction, dramatic form changes to house its people.

Waiting for Godot is structured in symmetry since the theme lies imbedded in Luke's account of the crucifixion: one of the thieves was saved, and one was damned. Didi and Gogo are two tramps who might be thieves; Pozzo and Lucky are master and slave who are another variant of thieves. Even Godot's boy has a brother; one of them minds the sheep and one the goats. Set and props bolster the human symmetries: a horizontal road and a vertical tree, a rope around Lucky's neck and one around Gogo's trousers, a dinner of chicken and one of carrot, business with hat and business with boots. The dialogue sparkles with the vaudeville duets of Gogo and Didi, but by play's end the duets have frozen to immobility, while Godot remains offstage, a mysterious and dwindling source of hope.

Hope wanes toward zero in *Endgame*. Symmetry is vestigial—in two high windows that look at the world, in two low ashbins that enoage a generation. In stage center is Hamm, lord of a shelter without amenities; revolving around that center is crippled Clov, who prefers enclosure in his cubical kitchen. The stage spareness is redolent of global catastrophe: life is nearing extinction and, with life, all that made it worth living —friendship, beauty, wisdom, mercy. What is left is pain, and death should be preferable to pain, but Hamm hesitates to end, and *Endgame* ends without an end. Hamm believes he is left alone, but Clov stands motionless at the threshold. The curtain falls on fixity rather than finality.

It is a critical convenience to discuss Beckett's drama as though it were conceived in uninterrupted sequence, but that is inaccurate. Not only did Beckett zigzag from drama to fiction, but he translated his

French fiction into English. Like Krapp with his tapes, Beckett subjected himself to old works "before embarking on a new retrospect." He evidently "relaxed" with a play after plunging too painfully into fiction. *How It Is* precedes *Happy Days, Play,* and the later pieces for mass media, and its imprint is noticeable. Like the narrator of *How It Is,* Winnie of *Happy Days* utters phrases rather than sentences. And like him, she treasures a few objects, even to a copious sack, container of objects. Like the narrator of *How It Is,* Winnie has a partner upon whom she depends for witness, for protection from the solitude she calls her wilderness. When *Happy Days* ends—with the habitual Beckettian immobility—Winnie and Willie look at each other in mutual witness.

All Beckett's plays close on stillness, but they move there differently—Krapp's listening, recording, and brooding; the intercalated monologues of *Play* repeated *in toto*; the realistic voices of *All That Fall* in contrast to the ghostly sounds of *Embers*; the struggle to create in *Words and Music* and *Cascando*; the flights from self in *Film, Eh Joe,* and *Not I*. Each work contrives its own rhythm: the play of light and dark, as of past and present, in *Krapp's Last Tape;* the light-provoked words in *Play*; the visual images that rise from the pure radio sounds of *All That Fall* and *Embers*; the blind antivisual strains of radio sound in *Words and Music* and *Cascando*; pure image in *Film* (broken only by "sssh!"); voice against image in *Eh Joe*; voice framed by mouth in *Not I*. Beckett feeds less and less to the senses as he continues to write drama; but that "less" is intensely concentrated.

So too, *How It Is.* This three-part narrative, told in free panting verses, influences the dialogue of the plays that follow it, but it is influenced by the stage couples that precede it. The protagonist that Beckett has called a narrator/narrated meets Pim in the central event of the book. But he in turn is met by Bom. He victimizes the one and is victimized by the other, à la Pozzo and Lucky, or Hamm and Clov. His story branches out to other couplings—Pim has a wife Pam Prim, Kram is Pim's witness and Krim his scribe (German *Krimkram*—"junk"). But unlike most couples in Beckett's plays, the members of pairs in *How It Is* can barely be distinguished. Each needs the witness of the other, but each couple might be the witnessed and witnessing part of a self. In Berkeley's Latin, *esse est percipi*, to be is to be perceived, and the self, as in *Film*, may split into perceived and perceiver. In a verse of *How It Is*: "and that linked thus bodily together each one of us is at the same time Bom and Pim tormentor and tormented pedant and dunce wooer and wooed speechless and reafflicted with speech in the dark the mud nothing to emend there." No, nothing to emend in this remarkably lyrical fiction, whose protagonist is the lowest common denominator of self-conscious, word-wielding being.

How It Is is divided into three equal parts, each introduced by an Arabic number, each with its own title hammered at us: "Before Pim," "With Pim," "After Pim." But the neatness is a ruse, and within each part we find the Beckettian narrator/narrated trying to order anarchy through images, through numbers, through preposterous story remnants rising from ubiquitous mud. Probably the most difficult work in the Beckett cannon, *How It Is* invents a language rhythmically if not lexically, a language that seems to imitate the body's movements through the mud and the mind's movements through its mud. Evanescent monosyllabic names yield a single idiom, musicalizing painful questions, musicalizing human questions. *How It Is* imposes statement on a question without answering the interrogative.

How It Is is Beckett's last sustained work. His later lyrical fiction is constrained into more stringent economy, rare in reminiscences of visible reality and rigid in exclusion of invisible reality. Since language has proved too blunt an instrument to probe being, Beckett sets about examining being clinically, on its limit-line, before it dissolves into surrounding nothingness. But even these examinations are distinct and distinctive —the earth of *Enough*, the hemisphere of *Imagination Dead Imagine,* the elongated cube of *Ping*, the cylinder of *The Lost Ones*. And for all the resolute objectivity, *The Lost Ones* and *Lessness* are rending; the one with its divided society and last speechless couple, the other with its indomitable little body willing an impossible future; the one with scientific sentences as dry as the atmosphere they conjure, the other with permuted phrases offering a hope of chance combinations.

Beckett never backtracks, and we may look forward to more unsparing spareness. The last mail from France carried news of another play, *That Time*. Inexhaustible indeed.

Beckett's canon has elicited highly sensitive criticism, exemplified by pieces in this anthology. Focusing on different works, viewing them from different angles, the contributors have responded to my invitation with these new reflections, not previously published. All the contributors have immersed themselves deeply in Beckett, and their essays are at once an appreciation and an illumination—the only criticism worth writing.

Kay Boyle

All Mankind Is Us

> *It is not every day that we are needed. Not indeed that we personally are needed. Others would meet the case equally well, if not better. To all mankind they were addressed, those cries for help still ringing in our ears! But at this place, at this moment of time, all mankind is us, whether we like it or not.* — Vladimir in *Waiting for Godot*

Sam Beckett and I met in 1930. All I knew of him then was that he was a close friend of the Joyce family, and I was acquainted with the Joyces—in particular with Lucia, for we both danced with Elizabeth Duncan's group—and I had heard the family speak of Sam. The night I met him I had not read his poem "For Future Reference" (published that same year in *transition*), which he dedicated to his "cherished chemist friend" who had managed to lure him "down from the cornice/into the basement/and there/drew bottles of acid and alkali out of his breast." Also, I did not know that Beckett had just won the Hours Press prize for his poem *Whoroscope* in a contest Nancy Cunard and Richard Aldington had sponsored. The Beckett of that time (and he has changed little) Nancy Cunard accurately and perceptively described as "tall and slim to leanness, of handsome aquiline features . . . a man of stone, you think until he speaks, and then all is warmth if he is with someone sympathetic to him. He is fair, with a direct gaze at times coming to pinpoint precision in his light blue eyes. . . . If you think he is looking slightly severe, this may be because he is assessing what has just been said, and his laughter and ease of manner are frank and swift. . . . He is very self-assured in a deep, quiet way, unassuming in manner and interested in mankind."

Sam Beckett has since told me that it was in the Paris apartment of the poet Walter Lowenfels that we met. But whosever temporary stopping place it was, I cannot recall the faces or voices of any of the voluble people crowded into the room. It is as if they were simply not there at all. But Sam's face and the sound of his voice have never left me, for we must have talked for hours, sitting on a rather fragile sofa, upholstered in striped yellow and black velour, like a hornet's hide. Sam says that he tried to tell me about Machiavelli's *Mandragola*, which he had seen a night or two before, but that I showed no interest in it. He wanted to make me understand that it was the most powerful play in the Italian language, the language with which he was so much in love. This part of our talk has gone from my mind, for the very evening we met, a friend we both cherished had been committed to "a place," an institution, a madhouse, and I was obsessed with my outrage over the human dilemma men call insanity.

The truth was that I didn't believe in madness, not for a minute and not under any guise. Even if I had been locked up in a ward with the allegedly demented, I would not have believed in that cynical appraisal of their ailment. I was of the simplistic opinion that love was the missing element, and it had not come into my head until Sam Beckett talked his good sense to me that love can be the heaviest of all burdens man is asked to bear. I had, until that evening in 1930, seen madness as an outside force, an actual sinister alien who moved slyly into the bodies and spirit of the lonely and unloved, into the grief and longing of those who were no more than innocent bystanders. I saw madness as a despoiler who forced his way in on the artless and the defenseless, and began hanging up in their closets his various disguises, then shifted around the furniture to his own perverted liking in the rooms of houses that had never been his. Finally, he rid himself of the books that were there on the shelves, and put in their place his own demented library.

I believed this until Sam Beckett described to me the true topography of the scene. I did not know then that behind him lived the irrefutable knowledge and the anguish experienced in his visits to the Bethlehem Royal Hospital in Kent, a mental hospital where a friend of his was a doctor. I did not know (and still do not know except for the revelations in *Murphy*) anything at all about the faces and voices he knew there, or the eternal rocking of a body bound to a rocker by seven scarves, that he could never forget. He explained to me that night in Paris that madness is a geographical location inside the self. As he talked, it was almost as if we moved through purgatory together, and he was quite modestly showing me the way out for the condemned, saying that just as there are deep, seemingly impassible crevasses in the static ice of a glacier which mountain climbers cannot cross, so between sanity and insanity lies a fathomless abyss that it is not possible to traverse either by emotion (love) or by choice (the free will). "Once one has crossed over," Sam said, "there is no way back unless a bridge can be constructed for the return."

It was doubtless that same night in 1930 that Sam made reference to the two poets, Virgil and Dante, who passed together into Hell's antechamber and found themselves surrounded by the troubled who had in their lives pursued neither good nor evil and were therefore displeasing alike to God and to the Devil. That was easy enough to understand, but what the structure of the bridge for the return would be was not so simple to visualize. Some pilings or masonry of its foundations were perhaps to be found in the third canto of Dante's "Inferno," but I couldn't be sure about that although it was certainly Sam (become Virgil for the moment) who was saying:

Here all misgiving must thy mind reject.
Here cowardice must die and be no more.
We are come to the place I told thee to expect,
Where thou shouldst see the people whom pain stings
And who have lost the high good of the intellect.

In that far century, Dante had asked of Virgil:

Who are these that seem so crushed beneath their plight?

And Sam Beckett (still in the grave voice of Virgil) answered:

These miserable ways
The forlorn spirits endure of those who spent
Life without infamy and without praise.

Norman Mailer once wrote in uncharacteristic humility that Beckett's work "brings our despair to the surface, nourishes it with air, and therefore alters it. . . . The last ten years have been part of the great cramp of our history . . . that cramp which will finally destroy Will and Consciousness and Courage, and leave us in the fog of failing memory, expiring desire, and the vocation for death." Both in his work and in his life, Sam Beckett has quietly defied that threatened destruction of the Will. In *Godot*, he began the construction of a bridge across the abyss, offering through unremitting work, sometimes despairingly, sometimes with wry humor, a way back for man's stricken, paralyzed Will. Madness is never an uninvited stranger who moves into the house of the lost and the lamenting, Sam Beckett said to me on that first night. It is simply the strapping, and binding, and handcuffing by man himself of his own Will; and Will is nothing more than courage by another name. Both Beckett and Dante repeated to me that in Hell's anteroom, the torture of the detained is to be committed to the company of those who, like themselves, were too cowardly (these are Dante's exact words) to choose one side or the other, or to speak out (again Dante's words) of their beliefs.

The line of action which Sam Beckett's life has followed, a progression of decisive choices, traces another way out of the anteroom of detention which Dante has described. Like Joyce, Sam mistrusted the various pressures in his own country, and although he was appointed assistant to the professor of French at Trinity College, he knew (as he has put it) that he could never settle down to the work of teaching, and after the fourth term he resigned. "I didn't like living in Ireland," he said. "You know the kind of thing—theocracy, censorship of books. . . . I preferred to live abroad." So he left Ireland, but was back on a visit to his family when war broke out in Europe in 1939. Of the decision he took then he says quite simply: "I immediately returned to France. I preferred France in war to Ireland in peace. I made it just in time. I was here [Paris] up to 1942, and then I had to leave . . . because of the Germans." The German army units entered Paris in the spring of 1940, and thus Beckett's casual remark indicating that he spent two years there under the Occupation reveals nothing at all of the peril and pain and actual hunger that he chose to endure. Of his work in the French Resistance, Beckett says: "I couldn't stand there with my arms folded." It was for others to say that he was decorated for his services to England and France.

It might be supposed that I would have, through the years, continued to learn from Beckett's patient and forbearing wisdom, but I did not. For instance, when I first saw *Waiting for Godot* in New York City in 1956, I insisted on interpreting it as an evaluation of France during World War II. Vladimir and Estragon in their eternal waiting for liberation were discarded man, man relegated to the gutter, which, during an occupation, is his designated place. When Lucky comes out upon the stage carrying a heavy bag, a folding stool, a picnic basket, and a great coat, it is clear that these objects are the property of the man, Pozzo, who holds him tethered by the rope around his neck. These are not the belongings of the slave but of the conqueror. Pozzo's directions to Lucky (the sign and symbol of a defeated people) are as clipped as military orders. He cracks his whip and barks: "On! Back! Up, pig! Up, hog! Back! Stop! Turn! Coat! Stool! Stop!" Lucky, the subjected, the shackled, has no choice but to comply.

Pozzo admits that he might just as well have been in Lucky's shoes, and Lucky in his, "if chance had not willed otherwise"; that is, if the history of the war had been reenacted and rewritten.

The symbolic meaning of the figure of Pozzo is further confirmed at the moment of his meeting with Gogo and Didi, at which time he shouts out his name to them. "P-O-Z-Z-O!" he tells them, but Didi is not certain whether he has said "Bozzo" or "Pozzo." There is no explanation as to why the average Prussian invariably pronounces "p" as "b," but so it is. As if this were not clue enough, Beckett sits Pozzo down on the stool that Lucky has carried and has him eat a sumptuous meal from the basket that has been a part of Lucky's burden, a picnic lunch that includes chicken. In contrast, Gogo eats a carrot fished out of the miserable debris of Didi's clothes, preferring it to a turnip. (Carrots and turnips, turnips and carrots, these were staples of the actual diet of the occupied under the occupier.) Pozzo dines like a king, like a general, it might be said, before the famished tramps and the tethered Lucky, the ironically named shackled victim, the abject figure of the paralyzed will.

When the meal is done, Estragon asks tentatively of Pozzo: "Er . . . you've finished with the . . . er . . . you don't need the . . . er . . . bones, Sir?" Pozzo turns the bones with the handle of his whip, and when he speaks the blood runs cold through the heart, for it is as if one heard the commander of an extermination camp saying: "Do I need the bones? No, personally, I do not need them any more."

In the second act, Pozzo, the tyrant, is blind (no longer able to see the vision of conquered, subjected humanity), for the liberation (in my version) which Didi and Gogo have waited for is now on its way. When Lucky collapses in exhaustion, Pozzo too falls to his knees, crying out for help. It is at that moment that Vladimir exhorts Estragon to act.

During the German Occupation of France, there was one hazardous way out of France and that was the clandestine crossing of the Pyrenees into Spain. In the last act of *Godot* (the second act, when a few leaves appear on the previously barren tree), Estragon says, "We'll go to the Pyrenees. . . . I've always wanted to wander in the Pyrenees." Vladimir says: "You'll wander in them," but although they know that "down in the hole, lingeringly, the grave-digger puts on the forceps," still they do not, cannot go. "Hope deferred maketh the something sick," quotes Vladimir from *Proverbs*, but he cannot remember the conclusion, "but when the desire cometh, it is a tree of life."

When I submitted this *explication de texte* to Beckett in 1957, he said there wasn't a word of truth in it, but he has never held that or anything else against me.

Hugh Kenner

Shades of Syntax

We commence, so to speak, in the void, with an example that has acquired talismanic virtue in Beckett criticism, though no one, to my knowledge, has ever validated its credentials. Our one report ascribes it to St. Augustine, and has Beckett calling its pattern beautiful in English but still more beautiful in the Latin: "Do not despair: one of the thieves was saved; do not presume: one of the thieves was damned." Whatever the provenance of this, we have the report that Beckett was interested not in its doctrine but in its shape: "It is the shape that matters."

So let us look at its shape. An injunction; an example; a contrary injunction; a contrary example. So example cancels example, and injunction injunction. Or a different description: six words answer three, and six again answer three again, and one set of three is made into the other, its opposite, by a change of one word only, and one set of six is made into its opposite likewise by changing one word more. To complete the pattern, balance the equation, we need all eighteen words, no more, no less. Their symmetry appears to be perfect, their sum therefore zero.

And yet it is not zero, since the pattern exists. Although we may be uncertain what advice we have received from the preacher, though he appears to have divided the moral universe between despair and its opposite and then forbidden us either, yet he has not said nothing, because it is not as though there had been no saying. Speech, whatever its tampering with its own content, can never be equivalent to silence, and on reflection we grow persuaded that we have in fact been told something of importance, though something the words do not say: that since we are neither to presume nor to despair, we are to cultivate a habit described by neither of these. The field of the sentence is divided, canceled, and discarded; the field of moral possibility, to which the sentence hopes to lift our attention, is not divided in a similar way. So zero yields more than itself. If we want to see Beckett engaged in similar rituals, we have only to turn to *Watt*, where we find him on page after page dispensing a minimum of information in what the exasperated reader may feel is a maximum of wordage, and yet gratifying us with symmetries of self-cancellation which (formal however little they inform) leave behind them odd residues of quasi-meaning.

> Mrs. Gorman called every Thursday, except when she was indisposed. Then she did not call, but stayed at home, in bed or in a comfortable chair, before the fire, if the weather was cold, and by the open window, if the weather was warm, and, if the weather was neither cold nor warm, by the closed window or before the empty hearth. So Thursday was the day that Watt preferred to all other days. Some prefer Sunday, others Monday, others Tuesday, others Wednesday, others Friday, others Saturday. But Watt preferred Thursday, because Mrs. Gorman called on Thursday. (*Watt*, 139–40)

This ends just where it began, with the statement that Mrs. Gorman called on Thursdays, but in saying this twice it contrives to say somewhat less than if one saying had been sufficient. En route to the second saying, it contrives to empty from her Thursday call a surprising quantity of substance. Or no, that is not quite right, it devotes most of its attention to her Thursday non-calls. But let us particularize.

Thursday is exhibited as one day among seven days, differing from one another only in possessing different names, and as offering occasion for apparently trivial preference. Watt's occasion is the visit of Mrs. Gorman, which does no more, so far as we can tell, than distinguish Thursday from the six other days. Moreover, she did not really call every Thursday; she called "every Thursday, except when she was indisposed." So there are orderly lists in this world, and also bodily indispositions, one supposes less orderly. On such occasions, whose frequency is not specified, she stayed either in bed or in a chair, depending no doubt on her degree of indisposition. Finer calibrations are conceivable, but a bed-chair scale is the one we are offered. Other matters depend; depending on the weather, either the window is open and she sits by it, or the fire blazes and she sits by it, but if the weather cannot be characterized —which gives us a three-point scale for weather—then her doings cannot be characterized either. The window on such occasions is closed, and the hearth empty, but what impels her to nurse her indisposition by one of these featureless locations or the other we are not told and are left to guess that there is no telling.

This indeterminacy in the heart of the paragraph has made quite a show of locking its configurations into little symmetries of cause and effect, phenomenon and response, and yet has not succeeded in stating how Mrs. Gorman chose between a closed window and an empty hearth; this indeterminacy leaches outward, as we think about it, to affect her choice of bed or comfortable chair, to affect her state of indisposition or the reverse, to infect Watt's preference, to erode the very meaning of Thursday. Nor is this a casual erosion, since we next discover that on the Thursdays when Mrs. Gorman was not indisposed, and called, little happened except that Watt sat on her lap, and she on his.

So much can we acquire of a *Weltanschauung* by merely unraveling the symmetries of a sentence. If we are told less than we seem to be told about Watt and Mrs. Gorman, we are told more than we may think about the network of perception, desire, and decision that unites such actions as they do perform. The ritual symmetry of the *Watt* sentences in seeming to undo information chiefly undoes motivation, characteristically by rotating before us such an array of interchangeable options that no reason apparently remains why one should ever have been elected in preference to another.

But no, that is not quite right either. Motivation is not what gets canceled: motivation is never touched on. What Beckett posits, only to undo them, are systems of criteria. Someone—Mrs. Gorman or the narrator speaking for her (or perhaps consulting his own analytic convenience)—deploys a tidy system of binary choices (cold or hot, bed or chair, called or did not call, disposed or indisposed) which affects to map and explicate her doings but does not really succeed. St. Augustine's sentence in the same way offered a pair of options—presumption, despair—which it also discarded as insufficient. What is left when the pairs of terms are canceled, that is what was meant to arrest Augustine's hearers, and that is what haunts the mind of the reader of *Watt*.

This mode of purposeful negation needs careful isolating. There are many rites of negation. Here, by way of contrast, is another elaborate sentence with little of moment to disclose. It is from the seventeenth episode of *Ulysses*, "Ithaca," and Stephen Dedalus in the deep of night has been watching Leopold Bloom kindle a fire.

> What did Stephen see on raising his gaze to the height of a yard from the fire towards the opposite wall?
>
> Under a row of five coiled spring housebells a curvilinear rope, stretched between two holdfasts athwart across the recess beside the chim-

ney pier, from which hung four smallsized square handkerchiefs folded
unattached consecutively in adjacent rectangles and one pair of ladies' grey
hose with lisle suspender tops and feet in their habitual position clamped by
three erect wooden pegs two at their outer extremities and the third at their
point of junction. (*Ulysses,* 670)

This makes on the ear as grave and equable an impact as any
sentence of Beckett's. It is from the episode in which Joyce said that he
was telling everything in the baldest and coldest way, reducing Bloom
and Stephen to wanderers like the stars on which they gaze. Page after
page, trivia are equalized, equalizing whatever human matters they
touch.

And yet something quite different is going on from what we observed in *Watt.* The baldness and impartiality of the narrative are conveyed chiefly by rhythm and cadence. Rhythm and cadence are bal-
anced. But Joyce does not balance syntax in Beckett's way. "A
rope . . . stretched . . . from which hung . . ."—that is the kernel of
the sentence. The rest is amplification: where the rope stretched, between
what supporters, what hung on it, how the hung things were attached. At
the end of the sentence our attention is on three clothespegs and their
geometry. At its beginning our attention was on five coiled spring
housebells. Somewhere between, almost unnoticed, the sentence has
transacted its syntactic business, hardly to be noticed, save by analytic
effort.

There is no mathematic of self-cancellation, because there is no
returning to what would need to be canceled. The sentence does not turn
back upon itself, it merely moves in no particular direction. This is a very
different strategy of negation. When Joyce sets out to diminish and
negate, he does so in the manner of a man painting everything grey,
commencing somewhere and finishing somewhere else. Beckett works
by contrast like some methodical electrician, connecting the source of
energy to itself that the battery may be drained.

This principle pertains to more than negation. It isolates two op-
posed tendencies that inhere in the very act of writing, tendencies between which every writer must strike what balance his designs or his
temperament may dictate. Depending on the balance he achieves, he will
be either a word-man or a sentence-man. He is one or the other, of course,
by tendency only, since there can be no clear-cut case of either type. No
sentences exist without words, no words however jumbled can fail to hint
at a sentence. We can make out the syntax of *Jabberwocky* without
knowing what the words mean. Sentences and words, syntax and diction,
like so many pairs, they always and only coexist.

This principle receives less emphasis than it might. Writers, we usually say, are interested in words. They savor the sounds and interactions of words; they collect rare words. From Beckett we remember "viduity," "acervation," the etymology of "buff;" as for Joyce, he read Skeat's *Etymological Dictionary* by the hour. These are familiar observations. We are less apt to think of a writer as one interested in the shapes of sentences.

One reason for our neglect may be that many eminent writers in the last 150 years have in fact taken rather little interest in the sentence. It happens that Joyce was in this respect a highly representative post-Romantic writer, one for whom the sentence was by turns a device for packing words, or else a psychological mirror. Its formal structure seems to have interested him little. Here is the opening of "Ivy Day in the Committee Room:" two sentences about fire-laying:

> Old Jack raked the cinders together with a piece of cardboard and spread them judiciously over the whitening dome of coals. When the dome was thinly covered his face lapsed into darkness but, as he set himself to fan the fire again, his crouching shadow ascended the opposite wall and his face slowly re-emerged into light.

One thing that is not meant to catch our attention is the shape of these sentences. In the first, which tells us that old Jack raked and spread, the most emphatic word, the word on which the voice pauses, is an adverb: "judiciously." To swing a sentence round on an adverb is a device that Joyce uses frequently. It dwells on a quality, not on a specified action. And the second sentence of "Ivy Day" illustrates another favorite device. It has not one subject, but two: "face" and "shadow." "His face lapsed" . . . but "his shadow ascended." Two subjects, two verbs, a "but": unremarkable, but not orderly, that is, not the orthodox "but" of constructions like, "His head was large but his hat was small." The orthodox "but" balances assertion against assertion: something affirmed of the head, by contrast something affirmed of the hat. Joyce's sentence has no intention of arresting us in this way to examine a contrast. His "but" is a phantom "but." It does not contrast two assertions nor two states, it simply serves as a transitional device between two events that succeeded one another in time, a darkening, a brightening. This is not a contrast to contemplate, it is nothing but narrative sequence. "And" would have done nearly as well. Once we have spotted this principle, we can see that the subjects arrayed on either side of the "but" are no more than the narrative conveniences of someone setting down phenomena in sequence, the sequence you would have observed had you been there. In the same way, the sentence from *Ulysses* about the doorbells and the clotheslines and the drying clothes does nothing more formal than record the sequence of Stephen's observations. In both cases, some force external to the economy of the sentence is directing its activities. That force, not the tension system intrinsic to the sentence itself, was Joyce's prime concern, and he moved easily to internal monologue, which can do without formal sentences altogether.

Here is one more Joycean exhibit: a long formal sentence from *A Portrait of the Artist as a Young Man* which sets the stage for Stephen's interview with the director of studies: "The director stood in the embrasure of the window, his back to the light, leaning an elbow on the brown crossblind and, as he spoke and smiled, slowly dangling and looping the cord of the other blind." "The director stood": that is all its syntax derives from. Everything else is circumstantial: two more subordinated verbs, "spoke" and "smiled"; three participial actions, "leaning," "dangling," "looping." These things are grammatically subordinate, but only grammatically. The verb to which they are subordinate has no particular preeminence: it is simply "stood." What is apt to catch our attention is not the syntactic order governed by this verb, but one detail of that order, the sentence's final phrase: "slowly dangling and looping the cord of the other blind." He is inconspicuously offering Stephen a noose.

We might profitably traverse the rest of the remarkable paragraph that sentence opens. Again and again, as it proceeds, the main verbs are structural conveniences merely; again and again attention runs outward to some subordinated detail: the movements of fingers, the fall of a shadow on a skull. In fact the word "skull" is the most arresting word in the following sentence but one: "The priest's face was in total shadow but the waning daylight from behind him touched the deeply grooved temples and the curves of the skull." This resembles strikingly the opening sentence of "Ivy Day": shadow/BUT/light. Again its "but" does not balance two assertions, since we barely notice the verbs on either side of it ("was" and "touched"). The sentence has been contrived to efface itself until it climaxes on that grim word "skull": the syntax a neutral showcase for the word it produces. And this corresponds, as do many more details in the paragraph, to the fact that things are not as they seem: the fact that the director is making a studied show of friendly conversation, mustering all the while at the edge of his performance the forces by which Stephen is to be entrapped. The noose, the skull, the trap: these are the real themes, kept subordinate as the director keeps them subordinate. That is syntax used as psychological mirror.

In Joyce's world, things are never quite what they seem. We are to watch the conjuror's—or the director's—fingers, not wholly trust his words. We are to keep always alert for the little gestures by which men give themselves away: the mannerisms which tell us that Ignatius Gallagher, in "A Little Cloud," is not the model Little Chandler supposes; the rapt pose on the stairs which tells us that Gretta Conroy's mind is not on her coming tryst with her husband Gabriel, but on a dead boy conjured up by a song. Climactic actions always occur elsewhere: offstage, brought to our attention by allusion. Such a way of managing a novel's themes and events has its counterpart in a way of managing sentences: the main verb displaced from its pivotal status by accessory clauses, accessory phrases, delusively climactic words.

Now we can try to define Beckett's odd achievement, which is to move the mystery into the heart of the syntactic mechanism, encompassed and held by careful structures which sustain it, in all its evanescence, before our undeluded eyes. Let us watch him do this, sentence after sentence, in a passage of some magnitude. I quote from *Malone Dies*. The aged Macmann and the aged Moll are experiencing passion in a nursing home: "There sprang up gradually between them a kind of intimacy which, at a given moment, led them to lie together and copulate as best they could." This sentence has nothing to hide except the meaning of the word "intimacy," which it credits with "leading" them. Of a "given moment" we do not ask by what power it was given. Its idiom is Euclidean ("from a given point, to draw a perpendicular to a given line"), and if there is something it fails to specify, that is because the language of careful analysis cannot wholly specify either, where passion is concerned: "For given their age and scant experience of carnal love, it was only natural they should not succeed, at the first shot, in giving each other the impression they were made for each other." "It was only natural they should not succeed": that is the official kernel of the sentence, and also the import of the sentence. Two ironies attend it, the delicate colloquialisms, "at the first shot" (shot!) and "made for each other." These cliches import a note of falseness which does not at all undercut the assertion of the sentence, but reinforces its assertion: they were working at a mutual illusion and not at first succeeding, "but far from losing heart, they warmed to their work." Still crystal clear, though "heart" shrugs off connotations of Petrarchan passion, and "warmed" has less calorific than idiomatic import. "And though both were completely impotent they finally succeeded, summoning to their aid all the resources of the skin, the mucus and the imagination, in striking from their dry and feeble clips a kind of sombre gratification." Nothing, again, to hide: no peripheral raveling. "They finally succeeded": indeed they did, and with a success that transcends impotence. It is specified: "a kind of sombre gratification" (much like that of the sentence). Its agents are specified: "all the resources of the skin, the mucus and the imagination." All these resources: that is to say very much, and we gather that very much was needed and are not surprised to find "imagination" at the climax of this triad. "But on the long road to this what flutterings, alarms and bashful fumblings, of which only this, that they gave Macmann some insight into the expression, Two is company."

To be given words, to be able to rehearse words with facility, to acquire only by long effort, perhaps terminally, some insight into what the things we say so glibly can connote, this is not Beckettian whimsy but human experience. The novel we are quoting has a one-sentence title, *Malone Dies*, and Malone is not unique in not knowing the full meaning of this little sentence. "He then made unquestionable progress in the use of the spoken word and learnt in a short time to let fall, at the right time, the yesses, noes, mores and enoughs that keep love alive." That there is deflation here we cannot doubt. But it is not a deflation gotten, in Joyce's way, by switching us off the track of the sentence we are reading. It is achieved, with Cartesian formality, by balancing the keeping of love alive against four pedantic plurals: "yesses," "noes," "mores," "enoughs." How odd is the word "noes," seen on the page! How fragile, correspondingly, is love!

Beckett is no more indifferent to the single word than is Joyce, who set down the word "skull" by way of climax when he was presenting a priest. But the Beckett syntax keeps steady control over the apparition of such words. It does not, like Joyce's, permit them to surface at its fringes, in disregard of the formal syntactic business that is being transacted. Such words, for Beckett, are intrinsic to the sentences' official business, which we may now try to formulate. The official business of the Beckett sentence is to affirm a tidy control it cannot quite achieve.

Neatly, foreseeing its end when it launches its beginning, the sentence offers to say what there is to be said, even when its theme is chaotic, inarticulate passion. Using its repertory of subject-verb-object relations and its authorized subordinating devices, it will map any relationships by which it is confronted. It will *say* them, and will say them all according to the one scheme: subject-verb-object. Such, it claims, are its resources, and therefore it is always in control. This is a very large claim, larger even than Newton's, who claimed that by pivoting various symbols around an equals sign he could map the course of apples and planets equally.

It is a large claim, and it is always falsified. It is falsified by some radical incompatibility between syntactic order and human nuance. Hence our comparative ignorance of Mrs. Gorman's Thursdays. Hence Malone's bleak phrases, "giving each other the impression they were made for each other"; "the resources of the skin, the mucus and the imagination"; "the yesses, noes, mores and enoughs the keep love alive." It is in its terms that the sentence is insufficient, not in its geometry nor its dynamics. In a better world, that wonderful dynamic system would have better terms to relate. In our world, it must relate mere verbs, mere nouns, mere colloquial phrases.

Sometimes Beckett achieves a chilling climax precisely because for once words do not fail, and the sentence itself, we perceive, is the agent by which the universe is emptied. Malone again, meditating on the responsibilities that attend the creation of a fictional character: "And yet I write about myself with the same pencil and in the same exercise-book as about him." "Firm," "central"; "I write about myself and him," samely. "It is because it is no longer I, I must have said so long ago, but another whose life is just beginning." I, dying, write about one who is (so to speak) being born. Then unforeseeably, in one of the great sentences of the novel, the two coalesce: the sentiment that attends the phrase "one whose life is just beginning," and the reality that is put forth by the title, *Malone Dies*. Here is the sentence: "It is right that he too should have his little chronicle, his memories, his reason, and be able to recognize the good in the bad, the bad in the worst, and so grow gently old down all the unchanging days and die one day like any other day, only shorter." "Only shorter": a guillotine phrase. And logic, impeccable logic, the same logic that guides syntax has produced it. "Growing gently old down all the unchanging days" is a process that precludes catastrophe, and the last day will (therefore) have the same quality as the ones that preceded it. Yet it will differ: will differ in duration. And the rhythm at the end of the sentence is what cuts off sentence and day with so appalling a finality: "only shorter."

That is a typical Beckett strategy, to equate syntax with logic, lull us with their coincidence, then trap us with the consequence. We may note a premonition of the shocking end, when "chronicle" leads to "memories," because if you have a story you remember it, and "memories" to "reason," because reason works on what memory has stored; and then "reason" leads to recognizing "the good in the bad" (a phrase we have all heard before in circumstances when we felt the person who quoted it at us was enjoying more reason than we were capable of), and symmetry produces that strange corollary, "the bad in the worst." Gently, reasonably, we have been moved by reason and cadence in cooperation to a point where the good is only what is less awful than any moment's norm. The effect resembles Winnie's "This will have been another happy day. (*Pause*.) After all. (*Pause*.) So far," a reduction anticipated by the opening future perfect and resembles too the recollection in *How It Is* of how it was: "in the dark the mud my head against his my side glued against his my right arm around his shoulders his cries have ceased we lie thus a good moment they are good moments''—good moments indeed, instances of "the good in the bad" if not of "the bad in the worst."

The business of a Beckett narrator is to order what he is narrating. That means, to frame sentences, to assert that tidy control. With each novel his plight has grown more difficult. The narrator of *Murphy* ("a million years ago") played facile games. If his sentences do not map quite everything, we must be on the alert to detect that fact, and may suspect that the narrator is deriving pleasures of his own from the little discrepancies. Thus nothing is easier than for him to specify Murphy tied in that chair, and to specify further that Murphy tied himself there. He had only to write down the words, with due attention to grammar and syntax. If he has thrown no light on how Murphy could have succeeded in performing this operation, well, many readers will not have noticed the difficulty, and those who have noticed it may guess that he has taken a sardonic pleasure in omitting a sentence there would have been no way to formulate. By contrast the narrator of *How It Is* attacks this kind of problem head on, and attacks no other. Where the sacks come from is a problem closely analogous to the problem of how Murphy tied himself into the chair, and it drives him through agonies of analytic attention, amid which he seldom succeeds in framing a coherent sentence, though his will is bent on nothing less.

That he is trying to utter sentences, and seldom succeeding, is a principal datum of this book. Memories will go into sentences, recollections of how it was: "the huge head hatted with birds and flowers is bowed down over my curls the eyes burn with severe love I offer her mine pale upcast to the sky whence cometh our help and which I know perhaps even then with time shall pass away." You can punctuate that, making it one sentence or two or three according to whether your taste runs to semicolons or full stops. There is no way to punctuate this:

> namely string them together last reasonings namely these sacks these sacks one must understand try and understand these sacks innumerable with us here for our journeys innumerable on this narrow track one foot two foot all here in position already like us all here in position at the inconceivable start of this caravan no impossible

This differs from Joycean "interior monologue" in registering the fearful effort to achieve coherence, achieve syntax. Interior monologue—the mind ticking over—exerts no effort to control its own contents; but the man in *How It Is* (perhaps named Sam, to fulfil the book's pattern of namings) is struggling to utter sentences, which means to control his thoughts, which means to grasp and comprehend the reality in which he partakes. Each block of type is a unit of his effort; we can gauge his progress by keeping track of the syntactic order he achieves. Nothing in the paragraph we have just quoted succeeds in even approximating a sentence. Four paragraphs later he has managed this: "such an acervation of sacks at the very outset that all progress impossible and no sooner imparted to the caravan the unthinkable first impulsion than arrested for ever and frozen in injustice"—no hesitations nor false starts, no "understand try and understand"; in fact a trim economical construction that has achieved all that we expect of a sentence except the incorporation of a verb or verbs. Verbs in the format "there would be" and "it would be" are readily supplied: grammatical fillers to render the syntax orthodox. The act of understanding has been accomplished: understanding not of the dark reality but of part of the problem created by his own previous efforts to understand and state it. This kind of second-level syntax, reporting the deficiencies that have attended first-level syntax, the syntax (the ordering) that is not localized in sentences but has inhered in the shaping, so far, of the entire narrative venture. Exactly like a writer who has devoted much effort to a story with a complicated plot in which, very late, he discovers a fatal defect, this unnamed struggler, this—so to speak—Samless Sam finds himself in the position of the reader of one of the symmetries in *Watt*, the passage about Mrs. Gorman's indispositions for instance. It was tidy, symmetrical, comprehensive; and now there seem to be things wrong with it; and now he has succeeded in stating what is wrong with it, and achieved a new symmetry of utterance which in turn . . .

Which in turn will be vulnerable. And if his content at the end ("good good end at last of part three and last") is inextricable from his satisfaction at having done what Malone, for instance, did not do, achieved his intended structure, then it is such a content as sustained Malone each time he achieved that orderly paradigm, a sentence. Sentence by sentence Malone made local order, to have it overwhelmed at the end by dissolution, "gurglings of outflow." The man in *How It Is* achieves local order seldom, but overall symmetry (three fifty-page blocks) at last. And his effort too is overwhelmed, as we look back, by all the grim data he has not managed to clarify nor explain. Still, the illusion of control brings him temporary peace, the peace on which the book terminates. Control which turns out to be the illusion of control, that, for the Beckett syntax, is How It Is.

Yasunari Takahashi

Fool's Progress

I   HIS BIRTH

The Beckettian fool was born in 1929 and delivered in the pages of *transition* 16–17, as the hero of "Assumption." That story has not been reprinted, apparently disowned by its author and certainly disregarded by most critics. This short story begins: "He could have shouted and could not. The buffoon in the loft swung steadily on his stick and the organist sat dreaming with his hands in his pockets. He spoke little, and then almost huskily."

We are taken aback by the abrupt images of buffoon and organist. Who are these mysterious characters? Where are they? Do the loft and organ signify the inside of a church? But then how can the buffoon be there? This wilful mystification, reflecting the youthful arrogance of a twenty-three-year-old author, is perplexing until we realize that the buffoon cannot be other than the first manifestation of the "clown inside," whom Malone will acknowledge some twenty years later: "[Within me] all alone, hour after hour, motionless, often standing, spellbound, groaning." And the loft can be no other than what will become the typical Beckettian scene—the inside of a skull, the hero's consciousness. Probably the organist implies the hero as musician of his vocal chords.

Thus the opening sentences of "Assumption" present the unnamed hero as a young man who has the makings of a clown but is reluctant to exercise his skill. His artistry is such that he can, when so disposed, impose silence on the noisy audience by a mere whisper: "Just as the creative artist must be partly illusionist, our whispering prestidigitator was partly artist.'' The equation of artist with illusionist-prestidigitator —or, in other words, the refusal to classify the artist by a high calling (writer, painter, composer) or a low one (music-hall comedian, circus clown)—is of crucial importance, for the hero of ''Assumption'' is probably a writer, or a would-be writer, like the young Beckett himself.

The story then tells of the hero's increasing withdrawal into a silence, which, far from implying peace of mind, results from his fearful efforts to stifle something. The ''something'' is variously described as ''that wild rebellious surge that aspired violently towards realization in sound,'' as ''the longing to be released in one splendid drunken scream and fused with the cosmic discord,'' or as ''his prisoner'' whose liberation he both dreads and longs for. We might also identify it with a death-principle, in which case silence would stand for a life-principle. This is a curious reversal, for one would normally connect silence with death and the impulse to scream with life. A life-and-death struggle is waged inside the hero, until the visit of the ''woman'' gives the victory to death. She seems to take away ''something of the desire to live, something of the unreasonable tenacity with which he shrank from dissolution.'' He finds himself ''unconditioned by the Satanic dimensional Trinity'' (i.e., the world, the flesh, the devil); ''he was released, achieved, the blue flower, Vega, GOD . . .'' But not quite. Dying as a sort of Dionysian god each night, revived each night, he was still left hungering ''to be irretrievably engulfed in the light of eternity, one with the birdless cloudless colourless skies, in infinite fulfilment.'' Finally comes the real end:

> Then it happened. While the woman was contemplating the face that she had overlaid with death, she was swept aside by a great storm of sound, shaking the very house with its prolonged, triumphant vehemence, climbing in a dizzy, bubbling scale, until, dispersed, it fused into the breath of the forest and the throbbing cry of the sea.
> They found her caressing his wild dead hair.

The story looks rough-hewn, and its cryptic but tortuous style defies the reader. What the style reveals, however, is not a slack-minded young writer but a mind feverishly intent on itself. A cluster of motifs will recur in Beckett's later works—including minutiae such as the pallor of the woman's lips and her green hat, chess, Vega, forest, sea, breath, solitude in an enclosed room, a Christlike agony, a yearning for Nirvana, and the all-important struggle between sound and silence, together with a resentment against "that Power" that has imposed this struggle upon the hero as an inscrutable pensum. All this takes embryonic form in "Assumption." Unlike this first hero, however, the later Beckett heroes will never attain Nirvana; they will do away with silence in one final dramatic scream. Or, to resume our theme, the later organists will not be able to strike a last triumphant chord; they will have to go on playing and whispering endlessly, permitted neither to stop nor to bang. Death will not prevail so easily, and life will consist not in pure silence, but in a never-to-be-resolved tension between scream and silence, between death-principle and life-principle.

And where is the buffoon? After the deliberate presentation of the hero as the artist-illusionist-prestidigitator, the figure apparently gets lost. It would seem that the buffoon has forgotten his job and that the hero inclines toward seriousness, thus falling an easy prey to the "wild beast of earnestness within," of which Malone will speak. In other words, the hero was created as a buffoon, but he hardly develops in that role. Both he and his narrators have much to learn.

Nevertheless, we have witnessed a unique scene. The great scream with which our hero died and with which he filled the universe might be a scream of the madness which has at last overtaken him, a cry of joy at the consummation of the real Nirvana, a big guffaw at the joke that is life, or an amplified death-rattle. But it is also the first cry, the vagitus, of the Beckettian fool-hero.

II HIS LIFE AND DEATH

The "Assumption," stated with cryptic "assumption," is that *the hero is an artist is a buffoon*, yearning earnestly for death and an Assumption, like that of the Virgin. Beckett's later works will convert the hypothesis into flesh and blood, will discipline the simple arrogance into a complex humility, and will prove the Assumption utterly impossible. These works will also show how the newborn fool will acquire proficiency in his chosen art—an arduous process that requires nurture of both the clown and the beast of earnestness who battles within him.

With *More Pricks Than Kicks* the fool enters his *Wanderjahre*. The hero of "Assumption" leaves his Proustian room to move about, though his name Belacqua, from Dante's *Purgatory*, implies a stationary nature. Belacqua's motion is curious—a "moving pause" that befits a clown; one might think of Chaplin trying to walk down an ascending escalator. The peculiar incongruity arises from the fact that the Cartesian *ens cogitans* lodges in the *res extensa* of the flesh. Physically, Belacqua is born as a Beckett clown, complete with spavined feet, weak eyes, decomposing toes, tumor in the neck, baggy trousers, and other grotesqueries inspiring sneers wherever he goes. Mentally, too, he is already a Beckettian *internus homo*, a "solipsist." As a Geulincxian, he scoffs at "the idea of a sequitur from his body to his mind," and the mesalliance of the two gives rise to humorous situations. The clown image is often evoked: Belacqua's marionnettelike gestures, his embracing the tenets of the laughing philospher Democritus, his view of reality as "agreeable odds and ends of vaudeville," his favorite "sottish jest" about a parson who dies a funny death at an amateur production of a play, and the accidental death of Belacqua himself on the operating table. The last is especially significant since the operating theater is deliberately called "theater," and the "theater-socks" of the patient suggest classical comedy. But Belacqua, the poor fool, struts and frets upon his stage and is heard no more.

Beckett's fool elicits laughter that is almost outside the Bergsonian categories. The pun, for instance, is indispensable, though Bergson frowns upon it as the least commendable of the techniques of the verbal comic. Most of the humor springs from a sense of radical disjunction between inner and outer reality, and this disjunction is undreamed of by a genteel sense of humor. It is this savage sense of absurdity which distinguishes *More Pricks* from other artist-novels; Belacqua cannot resemble Stephen Dedalus, much less the romantic Tonio Kröger.

The Beckettian clown is of course serious like all great fools, from that of Lear to Buster Keaton, who could have claimed, along with Malone, that they were "born grave as others syphilitic." And it is for lack of seriousness that Belacqua is criticized by the narrator of *More Pricks*: "I gave him up in the end because he was not *serious*." Belacqua is better qualified for the motley than the earlier, nameless hero, but he is still an immature clown because, paradoxically, he is lacking in earnestness.

The narrator's disclaimer of his hero also presents us with the problem of the relationship between the teller and the told. For how can the teller have the enthusiasm to spend nearly 200 pages pursuing a man whom he says on page 38 that he gives up? Unless he is doing something else at the same time. Belacqua is indeed a *persona*, an *alter ego*, which the still-young Beckett created ("a dirty low-down Low Church Protestant high-brow"), but Beckett knew the inadequacy of Belacqua as his *persona*—that he was "an inept ape of his own shadow," or, in a word, a fool. In criticizing Belacqua, therefore, he was criticizing his own inadequacy, secretly laughing at his own immaturity, his own lack of earnestness, which created such an inept *Doppelgänger*. Seen in this light, the bantering confession, "I gave him up in the end . . ." reemerges significantly; could the whole book be Beckett's bittersweet farewell to Belacqua? (For a long time Beckett would not allow the work to be reprinted, perhaps intending the farewell to be permanent.)

Murphy evidences an increased degree of seriousness in the hero. He is a still point around which whirls a pursuit comedy reminiscent of the Marx Brothers. But he himself is in search of a yet more central still point, the "third zone of darkness" or the "Nothing than which in the guffaw of the Abderite naught is more real." That the seriousness of his search has increased Murphy's stature as a fool is confirmed by the narrator who admits that he is the only character in the novel who is "not a puppet." Murphy thus becomes the first of the fool-heroes whom Beckett will later acknowledge as his. On the other hand, *Murphy* is the last work Beckett has written in the form of the traditional novel, the omniscient narrator telling the story of a hero who is surrounded by citizens of the realistic world. Also, it is the last work in the Beckett canon to grant the hero a quick death. A new form of fiction had to be created to tell a story of a hero who, neither a citizen himself nor in touch with realistic people, wanders endlessly, never permitted to finish.

With *Watt* we seem to reach an impossible nadir, a logical conclusion of the trajectory. The distance covered by the Beckett hero in his pursuit of seriousness, even to the point of insanity, may be measured by a comparison of the images of mental asylums in each work: there is no mention of such asylum in "Assumption"; Belacqua glances yearningly at the Portrane Lunatic Asylum; Murphy becomes an attendant at the Magdalen Mental Mercyseat; Watt becomes an asylum inmate. Watt's experience of Nothing at Mr. Knott's house is far more radical than that of Murphy at the Mercyseat, and the resulting disintegration of his mind places Watt in the same category as the schizophrenic Mr. Endon, who was envied by Murphy. The ambiguity of the word fool is exposed: gone is the fool-as-clown (buffoon) who, by pretending to be foolish, functions as an entertainer and often as a satirist; the fool is now mentally disabled—an idiot, a madman, or a schizophrenic. The passion for exhaustive permutation, which staggers the reader of *Watt*, would be classified by a pathologist like Minkowski as a "mania for geometric exactitude," a symptom of schizophrenia. But it is a curious victory of the novel that that same mania engenders an unprecedented kind of humor. The victory is almost pyrrhic, and the humor evokes a "mirthless laugh," a "risus purus," as Arsene calls it.

The fool blossoms into perfect maturity in the trilogy. By kicking against the bedrock Watt had reached, Molloy succeeds in rising out of the danger of insanity to emerge as a supreme fool, indefatigably tough and immensely resourceful, as if he had been cured in an asylum to walk out into the wide world again. Technically, this is facilitated through adoption of the first person singular, towards which Beckett had been groping through the Watt-Sam structure of *Watt*. Thematically, the hero, explicitly identified as a writer, has become a fool who consciously and professionally deals with language. The struggle between the clown and the wild beast of earnestness often takes the form of the interminable fight between silence and speech, in the greatest possible tension.

We now trace the last phase of the fool's progress. After full bloom in the trilogy, the curve turns downward, and the fool "much pines him away," in the manner of Lear's Fool after Cordelia's departure. Belacqua and Murphy could laugh at their own favorite jokes; Watt embodied the loss of laughter; Vladimir, too, his hand on his pubis, "daren't even laugh any more," but he could turn the very loss of laughter into an exquisite laugh, and so could Winnie, who could "magnify the Almighty . . . by sniggering with him at his little jokes, particularly the poorer ones"; but Harry in *Embers* (before *Happy Days*) can barely recall the laugh that attracted his wife. Progressively, even the laugh of the loss of laugh tends to be lost: the Man of *Play*, longing for the time when "all this will have been just play," never laughs; Joe never even smiles in *Eh, Joe*; the hero of *Film*, fittingly played by Buster Keaton, does not smile; and the fool disappears from *Breath*. One does not know whether to shudder with awe at the growing fierceness of the beast of earnestness, which apparently must tear its prey to pieces, or to marvel and rejoice at the tenacity of the die-hard clown who manages to show signs of survival at unexpected moments; e.g., the unaccountable yet funny sound "ping" in the otherwise serious text, resembling the effect of the hiccup in *Play*; or the Murphian vagitus repeated at the beginning and the end of *Breath*; or the brief laughs which both relieve and accentuate the withering pessimism of *Not I*. The greatest creator of fools in modern literature has evidently felt compelled to strangle the creature he has brought to birth and then to rare perfection.

III   THE TESTAMENT

To talk of the end of the fool is to talk of the fool of the end. As we have seen, the individual end, the personal death, was always immanent rather than imminent to the Beckett fool, and he has been playing an endgame ever since his birth—an endgame in a vast context. In Yeats' *A*

Vision, the Fool appears in the very last phase of the moon; Beckett's creation might well be this eschatological fool.

Beckett's achievement lies in reviving the tradition of the fool which, dating back to the immemorial past of folklore, reached its golden age in the Renaissance literature of Erasmus, Rabelais, Shakespeare, and Cervantes. And he did this against tremendous odds, for the conditions no longer obtain—social, ideological, and literary—which enabled those masters to create immortal fools; their society knew the living presence of the fool-figure, the audible echo of the medieval Feast of Fools, the sacred quality of certain idiots, the creative belief in a *theatrum mundi* (Everyman being a fool-actor in a divine comedy), and the healthy carnival or festive space, in which there was periodic reversal of the ordinary system of values. The Golden Age was itself a flower in bloom, a swan's song, for authoritarian efforts gradually suppressed the Feast of Fools. As Michel Foucault has demonstrated, the late seventeenth century saw the building of mental asylums outside the towns, so as to conceal madmen and idiots from the sight of normal citizens and to exclude the problem of madness from the consciousness of Cartesian man.

Coming at the end of this deteriorative process, Beckett's fool is deprived of his privileges. Although Beckett drew upon underground energies from *commedia dell' arte* through circus to silent film, he had no other choice than to accept the egregious contradiction in terms—a fool without festive space. And what he did was ironic; taking this Cartesian man who drove the fool-madman-idiot out of the acknowledged orbit of the modern world, he stripped him of his arrogant paraphernalia till he became a bare, forked animal and a fool-madman-idiot himself. It is difficult to read the beginning of "The Expelled," where the hero is hurled down the *steps*, without recalling from Beckett's early poem *Whoroscope* René du Perron "who has climbed the bitter steps." The wandering of the hero, thus begun, tended toward the "second starless inscrutable hour" for which the dying Descartes prayed.

Yet Beckett's work is anything but a facile satire on Descartes. Reading the first passages of *Meditations*, where Descartes tries to justify his exclusion of the problem of madness from the treatise, one might suspect that he saw the possibility of madness inhering in the very principle of rational thinking, but that the instant he saw it, he rejected it. Could it be that Beckett set for himself the task that Descartes chose to eliminate at the outset of the modern age—a descent into the depths to find his double in the figure of the fool-madman-idiot? And could it be that Beckett knew it was his own double? The identification is on such a deep level that one may tentatively call it a *"Deckett-Bescartes phenomenon."* *Whoroscope* may be a true horoscope cast at the birth of the Beckett hero.

Beckett's fool is an eschatological fool who appeared at the end of the fool tradition, a *homo ludens* at the end of the tether, enacting his own death, a prophet come to announce in his own person the death of the *homo europeus cartesianus*. In terms of literary history, he is eschatological in that he has given to European literature a radical push towards an end of a cycle, through his scathingly honest laying bare of the fundamental assumptions about language.

In the last analysis, however, the end is the end of the world itself. Even though it is only an alarm clock instead of the angels' trumpets that sounds, Hamm and Winnie are veritably in an apocalyptic situation; the spotlight that questions the characters of *Play* might well be Christ at the Last Judgment. And it is the role of Beckett's fool to laugh in the teeth of this situation. Winnie's serio-comic remark on God's poor jokes is one of Beckett's best gags, more—oh how much more—effective than Nietzsche's high-buskined *sententia*: "To see the collapse of tragic Nature and to be able to laugh at it—this it is that makes us equal to the Gods." We are reminded of Lear's Fool who survived the "collapse of tragic Nature" which destroyed the king's mind, but unlike him, Beckett's fool cannot disappear halfway through the play. He must go on laughing at and being laughed at by "the Unknowable," which Georges Bataille defines as the source of laughter, forever repeating his pratfalls, both physical and metaphysical, approaching ever nearer his own vanishing point but never quite touching it.

If Ixion makes a hero of himself by persisting in his inscrutable *pensum*, the fool will make a saint of himself by persisting in his folly. And gradually, in our own vision à la Yeats, we begin to see the image of the ultimate Fool of the twenty-eighth phase merge with that of the Saint of the twenty-seventh. "After us the savage God," wrote Yeats. Whatever may come after us, after the end of a cycle, in a *third* "starless inscrutable hour," we have in the whole oeuvre of Beckett a great Testament of the Fool, or a Gospel according to Saint Samuel.

John Fletcher

Beckett as Poet

I

As a poet, Beckett is a minor talent. To be less honest about his stature as a poet would be to invite skepticism for one's evaluation of the fiction (which I consider on a par with Kafka's and Nabokov's) or of the drama (which seems to me the greatest of any living English-language playwright). Beckett as poet is disadvantaged by an unfortunate though superficial resemblance to the richer poetic mode of T. S. Eliot. Both authors owe a great deal to Dante; both wrote the sort of verse to which publishers urged them to append explanatory notes; and both weave into their work allusions to their voluminous reading and to their private suffering. But there the resemblance ends. Eliot, the Anglican high Tory, contemplates with distaste the contemporary world and longs for a return of the golden age that he locates around the era of Lancelot Andrewes; Beckett, the lapsed Protestant atheist, has no such reactions against the modern world, since for him the greatest problem is our having been born, and that has been going on since eternity.

II

Of the dozen or so valid poems collected in Beckett's truly slim, "slim volume," nearly half are, perhaps surprisingly, narrative poems. It is true that they all date from the thirties, long before Beckett had begun doubting and subverting the very concept of "story" (as he was to do in his postwar French fiction); nevertheless, for such a reticent fabulist (or,

41

as Robert Scholes might say, fabulator) it is curious how much of his collected verse is in the narrative mode. "Enueg I" is perhaps the best of the group, and it runs to all of three pages. The title, like "Alba" and "Serena," is borrowed from Provençal or troubadour poetry, but Beckett's *enuegs* resemble those of the twelfth century only loosely. The early *enueg*—the word means something like "nuisance"—was a loose catalogue of items, some of them fairly scabrous, which annoyed or irritated the poet, such as "tough beef" or a "tight cunt in a fat broad." Beckett uses this free (in both senses of the word) form to itemize objects and concerns which bother or upset him, starting out with his "darling's red sputum" and ending with the fastidious reaction of his nose to a crush of "sweaty heroes" met upon the road. But he eschews the grossness and the triviality of the model and sets it more firmly within the fictional framework of a story told in the present tense:

> Exeo in a spasm
> tired of my darling's red sputum
> from the Portobello Private Nursing Home
> its secret things
> and toil to the crest of the surge of the steep perilous bridge

Anyone coming to Beckett's verse for the first time—indeed anyone coming to anything written by Beckett for the first time—might be forgiven for thinking this is mandarin nonsense. Mandarin it may be, nonsense it is not. The poet is writing of something that pains him personally to an extreme degree: the illness and suffering of a loved one which he has been impotently watching until he can stand it no longer, so that he flings himself out of the private hospital and starts on a bitter trudge around the suburbs of the city of Dublin, "my skull sullenly/clot of anger/skewered aloft strangled in the cang of the wind," biting "like a dog against its chastisement." Much of Beckett's writing springs directly from a private pain: but it is always well disguised. It is now known, for instance, that there was a "green girl" in his life in Dublin: she wore green, had greenish eyes, and was very Irish. Presumably she and Beckett—who has very blue eyes and is Anglo-Irish and of Huguenot origin—were fated not to succeed in their relationship. Was it like the situation so poignantly described in Joyce's story "Eveline" (in *Dubliners*), where the Catholic girl cannot bring herself, at the last moment, to run away with her sailor boy, who offers her an escape from the drabness and unhappiness of her life with her father? However that may be, years later, in the play *Krapp's Last Tape*, Beckett asked himself rhetorically, "What remains of all that misery? A girl in a shabby green coat, on a railway-station platform?" And later still, in the television piece *Eh Joe*, Beckett has the accusing voice remind Joe of his desertion of "The green one . . . the narrow one . . . always pale . . . the pale eyes . . . the look they shed before . . . the way they opened after." It is probably the same girl. Affectionately—but also as a disguise—Beckett gives her the name Smeraldina, which is Italian for "emerald green" (and Ireland, of course, is popularly known as the Emerald Isle). Lawrence Harvey tells us that "the Smeraldina" died at the age of twenty-four. Her death certainly overshadows "Enueg II" (in the line "the green tulips"), and she may be the "darling" of "Enueg I" since her green is turning "green-black" under the influence of the disease. The darkening, lowering sky shows up green-black, "like an ink of pestilence," as if the whole world were reflecting the cruel decomposition of the loved one.

The five lines I have quoted from the opening of "Enueg I" are therefore characteristic of Beckett's habit of masking his private pain in erudite but not necessarily obscure language. It is true that he expects his reader to have a smattering of Latin (*exeo*—"I go out")—in other poems of the *Echo's Bones* cycle he requires German, French, and Italian—but no more, and perhaps even less than Eliot expects of the reader of *The Waste Land*. Like Eliot, too, he plants a quotation from Dante's *Inferno*: "secret things" is a translation of *segrete cose*, Dante's expression for the shameful arcana of Hell to which his alter ego is about to be introduced by Virgil (*Inferno*, III, 21). Similarly Beckett's poet has left a "hell," the hell on earth of a terminal sanatorium. And again like Eliot, he speaks of a real place, the Portobello Hospital in Dublin's Richmond Street South, by the Portobello Bridge over the Grand Canal (a topographical feature that crops up continually in Beckett's writings); I am reminded of the Brighton Metropole and other real landmarks in Eliot's far from totally symbolic "waste land."

Thereafter in "Enueg I," Beckett explores his own waste land, and a drab and dreary place it is; the words "fungus," "oozing," "fetid" and "grey spew" not only give a somber emotive charge to the description of the landscape, they also elaborate the metaphor of eructation: the entire world is coughing up its pollutants like the "darling" her bloody spittle. All that the "wrecked" mind of the poet can do in these circumstances is kick against the pricks (compare Beckett's contemporaneous title for his collection of short stories, *More Pricks Than Kicks*), and end hopelessly with a citation from Rimbaud's *Illuminations*:

> Ah the banner
> the banner of meat bleeding
> on the silk of the seas and the arctic flowers
> that do not exist.

"Sanies I"—despite its title, which means "pus" in Latin—is less obsessed by corruption and degeneration of the flesh, though its treatment of the subject of birth is wry and slightly sardonic rather than cheerful (we could hardly expect cheerfulness on this subject from a poet who lovingly cites Calderón in *Proust*: "Pues el delito mayor/Del hombre es haber nacido," man's worst offence is to have got himself born). The birth in question is the poet's own; he recalls how he "popped" out like the cork from the champagne which was opened to celebrate the birth and slake the midwife's thirst, while his father ("the glans") took the day off with a friend from an insurance company. This memory is aroused by the fact that the poet, who is "tired now hair ebbing gums ebbing" and "good as gold now in the prime after a brief prodigality," is cycling homeward, to the house in which he was born "with the green of the larches."

Birth is also the subject of another long narrative poem, "Serena II"; this time it is a Kerry Blue bitch which "trembles . . . in the stress of her hour." Beckett, who once owned such a dog, recalls in this piece a long walk in the Irish mountains with it, and the fascinated disgust with which he was reminded by "this clonic earth" of the bitch's spasms in labor. This sets up a chain of images to do with birth and lactation (the harbor he can see below reminds him of "a woman making to cover her breasts"), but the horror of procreation—of the manner in which the convulsions of the act of love lead inexorably to those of the act of parturition—is brought into sharp relief by the acid phrase "the light randy slut can't be easy," followed like a refrain by the words which open the poem, "this clonic earth." If the reader was in doubt over the tone of that epithet at the outset, he is no longer so when he comes across it repeated in this context.

Of the medium-length narrative poems in the *Echo's Bones* cycle, "Sanies II" comes nearest to recalling the note of sour lament we associate most closely, in modernist poetry, with *The Waste Land*. The "American Bar/in Rue Mouffetard" is the kind of contemporary hell in which Eliot's barman shouts "HURRY UP PLEASE ITS TIME"; here a spanking takes place ("fessade à la mode"), and there we are told a sordid tale of the "pills I took, to bring it off." In Beckett we have a sardonic twist on Shakespeare's sonnet 116 ("suck is not suck that alters"); in Eliot we find the ironic juxtaposition of "Goodnight Lou" with Ophelia's exquisite and tragic farewell "Goodnight, sweet ladies." Of course to say how close Beckett is in this instance, to Eliot is also to point up the differences: a whole ethic is implied in Eliot's quotations and misquotations—most characteristically, in his ironic twisting of Goldsmith's pious lines, "When lovely woman stoops to folly" in the "typist home at teatime" episode— whereas Beckett's allusions imply at most a metaphysic, perhaps no more than an aesthetic. His poetry, unlike Eliot's does not indict the modern age as such; his allusions to the great writings of the past are not nostalgic hankerings for a past era when—as in the case of the typist's act of fornication—"stooping to folly" meant something. Beckett has no such generalizing ambition. His poem about his father's funeral, "Malacoda," draws heavily on the imagery of Dante's *Inferno*: Malacoda is one of the demons in the eighth circle. In Beckett's verses, he is an "undertaker's man," his perineum (unlike Dante's demon's) muted in respect for the widow's weeds; but his presence is invoked not to make an ethical point, but in order to link the poet's father with the "bulk dead" who are the subject of the other markedly Dantean poem of the cycle, "Alba." Significantly, "Malacoda" ends with a gesture of refusal, the word "nay," and it comes immediately after the spurious cheerfulness of "all aboard all souls/half-mast aye aye." This reminds me of the ending of the best story in *More Pricks Than Kicks*, "Dante and the Lobster," which describes how the hero Belacqua is baffled first by the fact that piety excludes pity in Hell, and then by the more homely—but for that reason the less acceptable—fact that lobsters are plunged alive into the cooking pot. Belacqua comforts himself with the reflection that "it's a quick death, God help us all"; but the narrator punctures this amiable dishonesty with the words that close the story, words that incarnate all the refusals of all the obscenity of suffering ever uttered by mankind down the ages: "It is not." Similarly the poet's voice whispers "nay" to easeful death at the end of "Malacoda." Beckett has an immense regard for Dante, as extensive as Eliot's, but unlike Eliot he will not embrace Dante's theology. The hero of *More Pricks Than Kicks* wonders seditiously: "why not piety and pity both, even down below?" Beckett's elegy for his father first assimilates the dead man with the bulk dead of Dante's vision, and then repudiates the sentence passed on them all. We are quite a distance from Eliot's fastidious detachment, although both attitudes derive from *Inferno*. For all that, Eliot is close to Beckett in the narrative poems of the *Echo's Bones* cycle; but the two poets have little in common if we turn to Beckett's short lyrics which are of distinctly higher quality.

III

The short lyrics are concerned with a number of issues: love, its extremes and paradoxes; death, either past or anticipated, especially of a loved one; mental torment; time and eternity; and what is called in "Cascando" (the poem, not the radio play of the same title) the agony of

"pestling the unalterable/whey of words." These cosmic issues of life
and art are handled in verse forms of great economy and concision;
Beckett's tight, enigmatic poems on these themes are usually worth all
the trouble it takes to unravel their meaning.

The extremes of love are the subject of two pieces printed appro-
priately vis-à-vis: "Alba," the subject of which is the Beatrice-type
figure of the maiden beloved; and "Dortmunder," which treats of a
whore, standing before the poet "in the bright stall/sustaining the jade
splinters/the scarred signaculum of purity quiet." Both, in their necessarily different ways, are love poems: Beckett has nothing (at least not at this
stage in his career) of Eliot's contempt of the flesh and its lusts; even the
somber phrase "mard of all sinners" (where "mard" means the same as
the French word *merde*) cannot entirely efface the impression of pleasure
to be had in a "night phrase" of this kind. The term "phrase" here is a
musical one; it is paralleled in "Alba," which obviously treats of a much
"purer" form of love, by mention of "the white plane of music/that you
shall establish here before morning." We know from *Murphy* that music
is a euphemism in Beckett's vocabulary for sexual intercourse: Compare
this sly aside, planted to allow the censors to "commit their filthy
synecdoche": "Celia said that if he did not find work at once she would
have to go back to hers [i.e., prostitution]. Murphy knew what that
meant. No more music." In this light we can appreciate the two forms of
love described in "Alba" and "Dortmunder": the one "white" and pure
as the title implies, the other "violet" and forbidden. If "Dortmunder" is
a veiled confession—and it probably is—it is also a defiant one. Perhaps
the Alba (Beckett's nickname for another girl in his early life) knew of
and condoned the kind of lapse recorded in "Dortmunder" from the stern
ethics in which the poet grew up: If so, this would explain the connection
the poet establishes between Alba and the Jesus who invited the scribes
and Pharisees to cast the first stone at the adulteress they had caught in the
act: like Jesus, the Alba "stoop[s] with fingers of compassion/to endorse
the dust"; and like Jesus's, this act of generosity cannot "add to [her]
bounty."

But such delicate allusions to love in its sexual sense—either as
platonic restraint or as venial debauchery—are less crucial in the poet's
mind than the consideration given to the problem of whether love is
possible in any sense whatever. The most extended exploration of this
theme is to be found in "Cascando," which—somewhat unusually for
Beckett—is a discursive, even a dialectical piece, pivoting round con-
junctions like "if" and "unless," and deploying rhetorical questions
such as "why not." Towards the end of the poem we find the poet's
dilemma in love summed up in this way:

> terrified again
> of not loving
> of loving and not you
> of being loved and not by you
> of knowing not knowing pretending
> pretending

This rather naive utterance gives way in the later verse to more poignant and forceful explorations of the theme. "What would I do," the poet wonders, in the third of the *Four Poems* of 1937 and 1948 originally written in French,

> what would I do without this silence where the murmurs die
> the pantings the frenzies towards succour towards love
> without this sky that soars
> above its ballast dust

and he answers his own question: "what I did yesterday and the day before/peering out of my deadlight looking for another/wandering like me eddying far from all the living"; those who, like the "lost ones" of a recent prose text, inhabit "a convulsive space/among the voices voiceless"; the voices which haunt the Unnamable and "throng my hiddenness." In such a world—in the drear limbo in which all Beckett's later heroes struggle to fend off the "silence of which the universe is made"—love is hopeless, and even "those with stomach still to copulate strive in vain."

But perhaps the most beautiful—and the most enigmatic—of all Beckett's poems about love is the last of the *Four Poems* and the one which closes the collection *Poems in English*:

> I would like my love to die
> and the rain to be falling on the graveyard
> and on me walking the streets
> mourning the first and last to love me

It is likely this poem—written not long before his mother's death—is Beckett's anticipated elegy on the woman who, he realizes as he turns forty himself, may well have been "the first and last" to love him. But it is no conventional lament: the poet, like Krapp in the play, waits in anguish, "wishing she were gone"; and yet in neither context do we have the feeling of callousness and cynicism. It requires a great love, a selfless devotion, to wish the loved one gone, removed from the misery and pain of sickness and degradation. And yet (the short poem's many paradoxes force me to use that qualifier twice in three sentences) there is at the same time a flaunted masochism, a defiant hint that the poet is no stranger to the pleasures of grief. And if the poem is about a mistress and not a mother, what curious perversity it reveals! As if to say: "I love her so much I wish to wallow straight away in the anguish I know I shall experience when she dies." He who has never experienced such complex and contradictory emotions amongst you, *hypocrites lecteurs,* let him first cast a stone . . .

Compassion, tolerance, a willingness to put his own head upon the block—these are the attractive features of Beckett's poetic *persona* (and, be it noted in passing, qualities conspicuously lacking in Eliot's). The tensions arising from the paradoxes latent in a piece like "I would like my love to die" are compelling attributes of a talent otherwise slender enough in verse terms. There are naturally not the same tensions in his two short pieces about death and bereavement, but the compassion is still much in evidence. I refer to "Da Tagte Es," which Lawrence Harvey convincingly explicates as another elegy, presenting "a vision of ultimate separation" from a loved one, possibly Beckett's father again, and the title poem "Echo's Bones" itself, which broods on the fact that the grave is the only real "asylum," or—as the opening sentence of the recent text *Lessness* puts it, "True refuge long last towards which so many false time out of mind." All other sanctuaries are a cheat and an illusion: in the earth, the poet appears to be saying—in direct contrast to Marvell's point about "none do there embrace"—man experiences the only "revels," albeit "muffled" ones, which are not a sham.

The sort of elliptical utterance we are presented with in "Da Tagte Es" and "Echo's Bones," where the subject is death, comes into its own in the poems which are primarily concerned with the theme of mental torment and suffering, "The Vulture" and "Saint'Lô." "The Vulture" adopts the same kind of ironic stance toward its source (Goethe's invocation that his verse should hover like a vulture in search of prey) which we have perceived in the Provençal-inspired poems: Beckett's poetic vulture drags his hunger "through the sky/of my skull" which is a sort of "shell of sky and earth," and the prey is unsentimentally proclaimed to be "offal." We are a long way here from Goethe's Olympian confidence in the art of poesy. But this 1935 piece is feeble stuff compared with the last poem Beckett appears to have written in English, *Saint-Lô,* which in my view is the finest he has written so far in either language (though the exquisite but as yet untranslated verses "vive morte ma seule saison" run it a close second), and which is cast in the form of a deceptively simple quatrain:

Vire will wind in other shadows
unborn through the bright ways tremble
and the old mind ghost-forsaken
sink into its havoc

Probably the only gloss which the uninformed reader needs on this poem is that the Vire is the river which runs through the Normandy town of Saint-Lô where Beckett spent some time after the end of World War II, working for the Irish Red Cross. The "other shadows" Lawrence Harvey interprets as being those that will be cast when the war-torn city is rebuilt and new walls produce new shade. However that may be, the general sense of the poem is clear enough: the town, which in rubble is a fair reflection of the metaphysical anguish the poet feels about life in general, a kind of objective correlative of his state of mind, will eventually rise again, and the Vire will wend its way through other shadows and different (yet probably not greatly dissimilar) forms of pain and grief; but the poet will continue, the more effectively for having been deserted by the "ghosts" haunting him in these ruins, to sink further into his own personal havoc, a state which no bombardment brings about and no bulldozer therefore can clear away. It is thus a poem about loneliness: the incurable sort that reconstruction and rebirth serve only to highlight and exacerbate. Once again Beckett is not callously indulging in a facile or glib cynicism: he is stating facts. Vire will wind again through a new Saint-Lô, but it will still be a place of shadows despite the fact that the "bright ways tremble"; as Hamm puts it in *Endgame*, "You're on earth, there's no cure for that." War is terrible, but life is even worse; the as yet "unborn" waters of the ever-flowing river are a deceitful promise of refreshing succor. Here Beckett's pessimism extends much further than Eliot's, since there is hope offered by the American poet that the waste land can be revitalized by spring rain. Beckett's attitude toward such a belief is probably best expressed in *Waiting for Godot* by Estragon's sour twist of the wise saw by Heraclitus, a philosopher from whom Eliot draws comfort, especially in *Four Quartets*, to the effect that one never steps twice into the same stream, that existence is a continually renewed and therefore potentially exciting phenomenon. It is hard to despair if life seems to be in constant movement, since better days may be just around the corner. Estragon deflates such happy optimism when he asserts, with characteristic forthrightness, "It's never the same pus from one second to the next."

Such "long shifting thresholds" and their deceptive comforts are the subject of the second of the *Four Poems*, "my way is in the sand flowing," which like "Dieppe" (a poem that links in paradox the words "again" and "the last ebb") wrestles with the enigma of time and eternity, though hardly as poignantly or as forcefully as *Malone Dies*, the novel which raises so acutely the issue of what constitutes living and dying, and whether the two states do not fade into each other ("It's vague, life and death", Malone thinks). But such abstract metaphysical notions are rarely a suitable topic for poetry, as Eliot shows in *Four Quartets*, from which one best remembers graphic images like the brown-edged concrete of the dry pool rather than the more prosaic meditative sequences. So, in Beckett's most didactic poem, "Cascando," what strikes the reader most forcibly is not the scholastic tossing-about of question and answer that I referred to earlier, but a fine image. Apart from its intrinsic evocative qualities it is a good fragment to end on, since it expresses limpidly and concisely the essential subject of all Beckett's better verse and indeed of his entire oeuvre: that the artist is condemned to a task of Sisyphean proportions, the obligation to say the unsayable and seek words for an experience which it is beyond the power of language to utter. In such circumstances what else can the artist do, Beckett wonders in "Cascando," but grind on remorselessly, "pestling the unalterable/whey of words?"

What indeed? Especially when Dante Alighieri, the revered *maestro di color che sanno*, the "master of those that know" (Dante's description of Aristotle which Beckett applies to Dante himself), ends his great poem on a similar note. "Just as the geometer must fail in his attempt to square the circle," Dante writes, "the description of the glorious vision of God which I was vouchsafed was a flight for which my wings were not fledged"; but, "On my desire and will prevailed the Love that moves the sun and the other stars." Such Love is tragically absent in Beckett's world: but the pressing need of it, to enable man to transcend his condition and his language, remains entire and unfulfilled.

H. Porter Abbott

King Laugh: Beckett's Early Fiction

> *Oh, friend John, it is a strange world, a sad world full of miseries, and woes, and troubles; and yet when King Laugh come he make them all dance to the tune he play. Bleeding hearts, and dry bones of the churchyard, and tears that burn as they fall—all dance together to the music that he make with that smileless mouth of him. And believe me, friend John, that he is good to come, and kind.—Dracula*

Samuel Beckett's first book of fiction was published in 1934 and took its title, *More Pricks Than Kicks*, from the Lord's admonition to Saul on the road to Damascus ("I am Jesus whom thou persecutest: it is hard for thee to kick against the pricks," *Acts*, 9:5). It is an odd clutch of ten stories, tenuously connected by the continual presence of a "kind of cretinous Tom Jones," a protagonist (if we can call him such) who is at once cynical and sentimental, indolent, erratic, fiercely attached to his eccentric habits, sensual, and Irish. His name is Belacqua Shuah, and we watch his life in Dublin and its environs. The book itself reads like an attempt to kick all the pricks. It is a plague on everybody's house, including the house of fiction, so that Belacqua's inability to act with plausible consistency is matched by the book's failure to live up to its half-hearted masquerade of coherence.

Early in *David Copperfield*, Dickens introduces a paragraph foreshadowing the sad fate of Emily. Then, with full respect for the seriousness of his craft, he has David express a discreet apology: "This

may be premature. I have set it down too soon, perhaps. But let it stand.''
The lines stuck in Beckett's memory, and in his first book of fiction, to
conclude a foreshadowing that foreshadows nothing of any importance he
remarks: "This may be premature. We have set it down too soon,
perhaps. Still, let it bloody well stand.'' Clearly this is an author who
does *not* care. He writes often as if he were coerced, as if the book itself
did not want to get borne.

Perhaps the closest successful model for Beckett's apparent indifference to success is Sterne's *Tristram Shandy*. Shandy's inability to tell
the story of his life the way it ''ought'' to be told, his repeated failure to
meet the formal obligations of his craft, became a *new* formal obligation
of a uniquely literary pursuit. His enterprise was a success because he
created his own audience who loved him as he loved it. But the author of
More Pricks than Kicks is neither warm nor gentle. His tone may derive in
part from the cold aesthetic elitism which is one of the differences
between Beckett's literary milieu and Sterne's. Beckett's major contact
in this milieu during the 1920s was James Joyce, a model of ascetic
dedication to his calling. Joyce's work had by then achieved the status of
a new and persecuted faith, and Beckett defended it with holy zeal in the
lead essay of a volume of devotional essays on the future *Finnegans Wake*
(*Our Exagmination round his Factification for Incamination of Work in
Progress*, 1929). The spirit in which he chides the reading public in that
volume is not far from the often pointed indifference to his public's
expectations which pervades *More Pricks*. But the emerging poetics of
incompetence that one can see behind this book is basically, despite
Beckett's elegant and densely textured style, a rejection of Joyce's
enthusiastic display of mastery. Beckett's wilful disorganization of his
craft arises from a vision of disorganization in life. As he notes,
Belacqua's ''apparent gratuity of conduct . . . may perhaps with some
justice be likened to the laws of nature.''

If the main object of this strange bag of tricks is to attack the
traditional pretensions of fictional form, the peculiar spirit of play with
which it is conducted suggests an additional object. At the end of the
book, Beckett introduces a cemetery groundsman, a kind of genius of the
piece, or at least of its conclusion, who presides over Belacqua's burial.

> He had lost all interest in the shabby mysteries. He was beyond caring. He
> strained his ear for the future, and what did he hear? All the ancient
> punctured themes recurring, creeping up the treble out of sound. Very well.
> Let the essence of his being stay where it was, in liquor and liquor's
> harmonics, accepted gladly as the ultimate expression of his non-chalance.
> He rose and made his water agin a cypress.

The passage is something of a blind, for Beckett's own nonchalance during the course of this book often manifests itself with a paradoxical strenuousness, as if the author were determined to play. It belies a certain "interest in the shabby mysteries."

One can account for this by turning to one of the book's rare dark moments. This is Beckett's startlingly good rendering of the death of a lobster, which concludes the first story. Belacqua has brought his aunt the lobster to cook for their supper. To his horror he discovers that it is still alive.

> "What are you going to do?" he cried.
> "Boil the beast" she said, "What else?"
> "But it's not dead" protested Belacqua "you can't boil it like that."
> She looked at him in astonishment. Had he taken leave of his senses?
> "Have sense" she said sharply, "lobsters are always boiled alive. They must be." She caught up the lobster and laid it on its back. It trembled. "They feel nothing" she said.
> In the depths of the sea it had crept into the cruel pot. For hours, in the midst of its enemies, it had breathed secretly. It had survived the Frenchwoman's cat and his witless clutch. Now it was going alive into scalding water. It had to. Take into the air my quiet breath.
> Belacqua looked at the old parchment of her face, grey in the dim kitchen.
> "You make a fuss" she said angrily "and upset me and then lash into it for your dinner."
> She lifted the lobster clear of the table. It had about thirty seconds to live.
> "Well," thought Belacqua, "it's a quick death, God help us all."
> It is not.

A shabby mystery, perhaps, but a painful one that makes sound logic of Beckett's determination to have fun in the rest of his book.

When it comes time for Belacqua's own death, there is no possibility of becoming absorbed in such empathy. Belacqua, lying on his hospital bed, trying to prepare his mind for the coming surgical operation (two actually: one on his neck, the other on his toe), finds help in Donne's paradox: "*Now among our wise men, I doubt not but many would be found, who would laugh at Heraclitus weeping, none which would weep at Democritus laughing.*" To give him additional assistance, Beckett sends an "angel of the Lord" to tell him the funny story about the parson with a bit part in an amateur production.

> All he had to do was to snatch at his heart when the revolver went off, cry "By God! I'm shot!" and drop dead. The parson said certainly, he would be

most happy, if they would have no objection to his drawing the line at "By God!" on such a secular occasion. He would replace it, if they would have no objection, by "Mercy!" or "Upon my word!" or something of that kind. "Oh my! I'm shot!" how would that be? But the production was so amateur that the revolver went off indeed and the man of God was transfixed. "Oh!" he cried "oh . . . ! . . . By CHRIST! I *am* SHOT!"

Belacqua laughs till he cries. Prepared in body and soul, ready to play his part, he swaggers into the operating theater and bounces up onto the table. But, alas, the production is shamefully amateur, and the patient is killed rather than cured: "By Christ! he did die! They had clean forgotten to auscultate him!"

By incorporating the death of his protagonist into a joke, the author baldly rejects the grimness he evoked in recounting the death of a lobster. Both deaths are absurd, but the death of the human character is elaborately contrived. It is not simply humorous, it is a joke, the author's own wilful derangement of reality. He asserts the illusion, at least, of control and of immunity from such tears as Heraclitus might weep. To sustain the joke, Beckett caps Belacqua's death with a final chapter in which he recounts Belacqua's interment and at the same time the carnal love of his widow and his best friend. The price one pays for this wit is a cold disengagement from people. One mocks death by mocking life.

This can be blown out of proportion. *More Pricks than Kicks* is many things, including successful satire of certain contemporary types, casual jokes which are just that—casual—showing off, and, as we have noted, a broad-ranging attack on the received pretensions of fiction to imitate life's mysteries. But the laughter of personal disengagement that Beckett evokes in this volume deserves emphasis and bears comparison to the kind of laughter evoked in his next book.

Murphy appeared four years later. In contrast to *More Pricks*, it is the genuine article, a novel. It has plot, indeed two plots, which in itself is a remarkable achievement by the man who made the repudiation of plot and character so much a part of the modern literary landscape. The plots concern on the one hand Murphy's private quest for happiness and on the other hand four characters for whom happiness depends on finding Murphy. Murphy is a Belacqua-like Irishman in London ostensibly seeking his fortune but actually avoiding it as best he can. He is bent instead on achieving a perfect autonomy of inner peace—a state he approaches by periodically strapping himself naked to a rocking chair. In his chair, he passes through what he imagines to be three zones of his mind until in the last he has become "a mote in the dark of absolute freedom.'' But Murphy also falls in love with a remarkably sympathetic early Beckett character, a prostitute named Celia, who urges him to seek employment. Through a chance meeting with the ''independent'' Austin Ticklepenny, he lands a job as male nurse (Ticklepenny's replacement) at the Magdalen Mental Mercyseat. Murphy discovers in its inmates ''that self-immersed indifference to the contingencies of the contingent world which he had chosen for himself as the only felicity.'' Surrounded by such models of human happiness, Murphy hopes to reconcile the demands of the public and private worlds.

The four who seek him are Miss Counihan, Murphy's original intended for whose sake he set out for London in the first place; Neary, Murphy's ex-tutor who is in love with Miss Counihan, but whose success in love depends on finding (bad) news of Murphy; Cooper, Neary's feebleminded agent whom he sends to London in quest of this news; and Wylie, also an ex-student of Neary's, who persuades Neary to seek Murphy himself. With Neary in London, Wylie satisfies Miss Counihan's lust and, to achieve the same end Neary hoped to achieve, bribes Cooper to switch his allegiance. The four eventually converge in London where they join forces. Alas, by the time they finally catch up with Murphy he has been burned to death in a ridiculous accident.

The two plots are developed in alternating chapters with the story of Murphy dominating. Their relationship is that of figure and ground, so that Murphy is more distinctly separated than Belacqua from the flat grotesques who epitomize the herd. He is also more distinctly a hero than was his forerunner— a vigorous development of a possible novelistic type, equipped with an idea about happiness and how to pursue it. The idea is augured briefly in *More Pricks* when Beckett describes Belacqua as ''an indolent bourgeois poltroon, very talented up to a point, but not fitted for private life in the best and brightest sense, in the sense to which he referred when he bragged of how he furnished his mind and lived there, because it was the last ditch when all was said and done.''

The ''private world'' here alluded to is a world Murphy would appear to enter, furnishing his mind and living there for certain periods of time. As a result, Murphy's story, in contrast to Belacqua's, is built on a clearly defined conflict between the pleasures of the mind and the demands of the world outside it (employment and his body's love for Celia). This difference in focus, with its sympathetic attention to what can actually be called a protagonist, affects the humor in the novel. The chapters devoted to the characters in search of Murphy have much of the traditional bite of satire. Murphy, with his larger understanding, is a ready standard of their failure to appreciate the rewards of the private world. This division into opposing camps often diminishes the special detachment we have observed in Beckett's early humor and generates at times a good deal of authorial engagement, including a direct attack on "the complacent scientific conceptualism that made contact with outer reality the index of mental well-being."

But as the time approaches for Murphy's death, the author reverts to the same cold re-creative play which he employed to dispose of Belacqua. In *Murphy*, however, the author's laughing disengagement from his central figure and the species of joke through which he attains it find reinforcement in Murphy's own ideas. Author and protagonist appear to come together in the same enterprise. Murphy, for example, is given to classifying experience "into jokes that had once been good jokes and jokes that had never been good jokes." Thus all experience is a matter of stale jokes or bad ones, and Murphy loves to excess what he considers a good joke. "Why did the barmaid champagne? Because the stout porter bitter." Murphy's enthusiasm for this joke is marked by analytical zeal. Choking with laughter, he imagines the scene.

> On the one hand the barmaid, fresh from the country, a horse's head on a cow's body, her crape bodice more a W than a V, her legs more an X than an 0, her eyes closed for the sweet pain, leaning out through the hatch of the bar parlour. On the other the stout porter, mounting the footrail, his canines gleaming behind a pad of frothy whisker.

The appeal of this "good" joke is the way in which its puns require the development of a new world in which stout porters bite barmaids. For Murphy it is an improvement on the world he knows ("What but an imperfect sense of humour could have made such a mess of chaos?"). Its pleasures of recreation are like those of the first zone of Murphy's mind—a parody of Dante's *Inferno* where Murphy enjoys "the pleasures of reversing the physical experience":

> Here the kick the physical Murphy received, the mental Murphy gave. It was the same kick, but corrected as to direction. Here the chandlers were available for slow depilation, Miss Carridge for rape by Ticklepenny, and so on. Here the whole physical fiasco became a howling success.

The ultimate in glacial comic repose is figured in a gentle schizophrenic named Mr. Endon whom Beckett places within the Magdalen Mental Mercyseat. His blissful insulation from "outer reality"—sexual, public, and rational—symbolizes for Murphy the object of his own quest. But Mr. Endon's spirit of play far transcends Murphy's feeble jokes. The cruel indifference of his play is sharply portrayed the first time Murphy goes on night duty:

Murphy found [Mr. Endon] in the south transept, gracefully stationed before the hypomaniac's pad, ringing the changes on the various ways in which the indicator could be pressed and the light turned on and off. Beginning with the light turned off to begin with he had: lit, indicated, extinguished; lit, extinguished, indicated; indicated, lit, extinguished. Continuing then with the light turned on to begin with he had: extinguished, lit, indicated; extinguished, indicated, lit; indicated, extinguished and was seriously thinking of lighting when Murphy stayed his hand.

The hypomaniac bounced off the walls like a bluebottle in a jar.

Mr. Endon is a deity unmoved by the plight of his creature. He controls the hypomaniac's universe according to a precise "amental pattern" and derives his joy solely from the combinations.

Murphy is as incapable of achieving Mr. Endon's asystematic play as he is his autonomy. He even falls in love with Mr. Endon, and though his love is "of the purest possible kind, exempt from the big world's precocious ejaculations of thought, word and deed," it is love nevertheless and as such exceeds the placid indifference of Mr. Endon. "Mr. Endon would have been less than Mr. Endon if he had known what it was to have a friend; and Murphy more than Murphy if he had not hoped against his better judgement that his feeling for Mr. Endon was in some small degree reciprocated." Recognizing his inability to purge this desire for personal connection, Murphy prepares to leave the MMM and go back to Celia.

At this point the author proceeds to destroy Murphy. Actually, killing him off is a practical joke Beckett prepared when Murphy first moved into his garret at the asylum. Murphy had demanded adequate heat, but Ticklepenny, instead of doing the obvious thing and installing an oil stove, had with great labor installed a gas heater. The heater was installed in such a way that the gas tap was located far off in the W.C. where it could easily be mistaken for a tap of a different sort. "It seems strange," the author remarks with ill concealed disingenuousness, "that neither of them thought of an oil stove, say a small Valor Perfection." The joke is sprung after Murphy takes his final leave of Mr. Endon. Someone accidently pulls the wrong tap, and Murphy is burned up in his sleep.

The joke is then capped by Murphy's last will and testament:

> With regard to the disposal of these my body, mind and soul, I desire that they be burnt and placed in a paper bag and brought to the Abbey Theatre. Lr. Abbey Street, Dublin, and without pause into what the great and good Lord Chesterfield calls the necessary house, where their happiest hours have been spent, on the right as one goes down into the pit, and I desire that the

chain be there pulled upon them, if possible during the performance of a
piece, the whole to be executed without ceremony or show of grief.

And this is capped in turn when Cooper, to whom the job has been
entrusted, stops at a pub and somewhat later launches the bag containing
Murphy's earthly remains at "a man who had given him great offence":

> It bounced, burst, off the wall onto the floor, where at once it became the
> object of much dribbling, passing, trapping, shooting, punching, heading
> and even some recognition from the gentleman's code. By closing time the
> body, mind and soul of Murphy were freely distributed over the floor of the
> saloon; and before another dayspring greyened the earth had been swept
> away with the sand, the beer, the butts, the glass, the matches, the spits, the
> vomit.

Beckett's nursing of these comic possibilities appears an effort to
approach what Murphy also sought: the glacial play of Mr. Endon. The
parallel with Mr. Endon's games is strong. Beckett has the patrons of the
saloon actually play with Murphy's remains—"dribbling, passing, trap-
ping, shooting"—before sending them to their final rest.

But the book does not end here, and though Beckett perhaps goes
one better than Murphy in aspiring to the detachment of Mr. Endon,
toward the end of the final chapter his cold playfulness has pretty well
disappeared. Our last moments are spent with Celia in a poignant rendering of her isolation. Beckett follows Murphy's lead here, too, expressing
his own inability to abandon such a personal connection as sympathy.

Beckett's third book of fiction has been described as deadening,
maddening, laborious, boring, exhausting—none of which are wholly
false descriptions. But its defects are the defects of a wonderful experiment. Recent evidence shows that it was begun in Paris in Feburary,
1941, while Beckett was still an active member of the French Resistance.
When he fled Paris and the Gestapo shortly afterward, he took the
manuscript with him to Roussillon where he worked as a farm laborer. By
1945, *Poor Johnny Watt* had become *Watt*, and Beckett had laid the
groundwork for the radically new craft of fiction he was to refine during
the following half decade.

In *More Pricks than Kicks*, Belacqua, referring to the Portrane
Lunatic Asylum, tells his current love that his "heart's right there."
Murphy took up lodging in an asylum only to discover that where his
heart was his mind could not follow. But Watt becomes a genuine inmate,
and the difference this makes is immense. His condition, however, is not
the happy psychosis of Mr. Endon. He suffers instead from a kind of

excessive sanity: a desire to define, to locate cause, to find meaning, or at least a "pillow of words" to substitute for these ends. In contrast to Belacqua and Murphy, he is earnest. He lacks their wit and recklessness. Their acerbity and defiance are replaced in him by gentle passivity and constant incomprehension.

His story concerns the house of Mr. Knott, Watt's voyage by train to get there, his employment there as a domestic servant, and his departure. Knott's house has two floors and at all times two servants, one on each floor. The arrival and departure of these servants are strictly regulated. When a new man arrives, he serves on the ground floor, the ground floor man moves to the first floor, and the first floor man departs. Why and when new servants must be hired and old ones fired, however, is a mystery like almost everything else in this house. When the time comes for Watt to leave, he walks to the station and buys a ticket for "the further end of the line." At an unspecified later time, he is discovered in an asylum.

To compound the difference between *Watt* and the two earlier books, Watt is kept alive and his story itself is composed (or so it appears) in the asylum. Its ultimate source is Watt who strains to recollect and communicate what he can never understand to his friend and biographer, Sam, who is also an inmate. We are never really sure, however, that the narrative's patient monotone emanates entirely from Sam or only in part. To compound the problem, the book includes an addendum of unused material with the comment: "The following precious and illuminating material should be carefully studied. Only fatigue and disgust prevent its incorporation." Our uncertainty about the origin and purpose of this document is clearly calculated and echoes Watt's own bewilderment about what he has experienced. It is part of a broader attempt by Beckett to re-create in his literary form the confusions of his hero.

At age twenty-three, Beckett had lauded Joyce's *Work in Progress* as being "not *about* something" but "*that something itself*. . . . When the sense is sleep, the words go to sleep. . . . When the sense is dancing, the words dance" (*Our Exagmination*). *Watt* is a similar revolution in Beckett's canon, but given the fact that the "sense" now is confusion, the experiment had unique dangers of its own. An art that sets out to confuse is not art as it is commonly conceived, but its opposite. The point to stress here is that what Beckett seeks is no cheap failure but a precise rendering of states of confusion—not simply the fall but, in the words of a later Beckett creator, Malone, "the rapture of vertigo."

What happens at the house of Knott? Mr. Gall and his son come to "chune" the piano, a bell is heard to ring, a broken bell is found, Mr. Knott is discovered in a tree. Events of "great formal brilliance and no determinable import,'' they are the strange events of an hilarious form of gothic novel in which mysteries of horror have been replaced by mysteries of epistemology. After a night ride on a rarely frequented line, Watt journeys on foot through the moonlight until he reaches the house of his curious new master:

> Finding the front door locked, Watt went to the back door. He could not very well ring, or knock, for the house was in darkness.
> Finding the back door locked also, Watt returned to the front door.
> Finding the front door locked still, Watt returned to the back door.
> Finding the back door now open, oh not open wide, but on the latch, as the saying is, Watt was able to enter the house.

Though Watt has many theories to account for this event, he is never to know how the back door came to be open. Nor are we.

This and much else in the book is delightfully reminiscent of the stunning first section of *Dracula* in which Jonathan Harker, an industrious and highly rational bookkeeper, takes his own night voyage to the castle of his strange new employer. At the Count's front door he stands perplexed:

> I did not know what to do. Of bell or knocker there was no sign; through these frowning walls and dark window openings it was not likely that my voice could penetrate. The time I waited seemed endless, and I felt doubts and fears crowding upon me. What sort of place had I come to, and among what kind of people? What sort of grim adventure was it on which I had embarked?

Harker's visit, like Watt's, sends him to an asylum, as a victim of ''brain fever.'' And one might note in passing that between his escape from the castle and his entrance into the asylum, Harker had rushed into a train station where, ''seeing from his violent demeanour that he was English, they gave him a ticket for the furthest station thither that the train reached.''

Whether or not Beckett consciously travestied his countryman's turn-of-the-century masterpiece is hard to determine. But Beckett has transposed into a comic, epistemological key gothic techniques for working directly on the reader's ''morbid dread of Sphinxes.'' A rather significant structural difference between Stoker's gothic and Beckett's is that in *Watt* the mysteries are sustained to the very end. In place of the meticulous diaries and tape recordings of *Dracula,* we have Sam's sad little notebook in which he may have left out things he was told and included other things he was not told. In place of Stoker's impeccable chronology, we find such masterpieces of confusion as the statement that opens part four: "As Watt told the beginning of his story, not first, but second, so not fourth, but third, now he told its end."

The difference is significant because it helps define the mental distance of half a century between Beckett and a major spokesman of late-Victorian optimism. For all the gothic immediacy of its horror, *Dracula* is an energetic attempt to exorcize the intimations of absurdity and nothingness it evokes. What triumph it portrays derives from the firm conviction of its intellectual hero, Van Helsing, that "there is always cause for everything." Harker is restored to sanity when he is convinced that what happened to him "really" happend: "It was the doubt as to the reality of the whole thing that knocked me over." He gains a "pillow of words" that neither Watt nor we ever do in our experience of Mr. Knott. When Watt tries later on to put his experience of Mr. Knott into words for his friend Sam, he can only produce a series of negative paradoxes, murdered in pathetically systematic, orthographic, and syntactic reversals: "For time, lived so. Not sad, not gay. Not asleep, not awake. Not dead, not alive. Not spirit, not body. Not Knott, not Watt. Go to, came day light" (Ruby Cohn translation). His paradoxes strongly suggest the *nosferatu*, concretions of nothingness who are antitheses of both life and death, body and soul. But what a band of nineteenth-century Englishmen can overcome with the help of the scientific method, a technology of records and God, the poor Irishman with only his systematic intelligence must live with forever: "that nothing had happened, with all the clarity and solidity of something, and that it revisited him in such a way that he was forced to submit to it all over again." As Sam explains, "to elicit something from nothing requires a certain skill."

It is possible to see in Watt's lists of hypotheses and elaborate computations a satire on the kind of Western scientific optimism trumpeted in *Dracula*. Yet the ridicule of Watt's limitations is mitigated by the fact that the limitations of his world are also great. And though what we see of that world we see through Watt and his debilitated amanuensis, there is no indication that the world is susceptible to any clearer comprehension. There is no frame to make the ridicule of Watt crisply satiric. Instead Beckett has abandoned the direct attack on "the men, women and children of science" which surface in *Murphy* and has taken up man's logical and computative powers as a positive tool of his art. He employs Watt's dogged efforts to be logical to enlarge the mystery of events that refuse to yield up their meanings.

What Watt lacks is not better thought and perception but the humor to live with and appreciate his world. What he lacks, in other words, is essentially the laughter he evokes in us. In his volume on Proust which appeared a decade before he began work on *Watt*, Beckett spoke with enthusiasm of an art which not only restored to experience its genuine mystery, but which at the same time evoked in the reader the feeling of enchantment which is part of the proper response to that mystery: "When the object is perceived as . . . isolated and inexplicable in the light of ignorance, then and then only may it be a source of enchantment." In the warmer laughter of *Watt*, he moved close to that art. And there are moments when Beckett so blends the inane and the endearing that our laughter at this confused martyr appears more an attitude of humility than anything else.

> Continuing my inspection, like one deprived of his senses, I observed, with a distinctness that left no room for doubt, in the adjoining garden whom do you think but Watt, advancing backwards towards me. His progress was slow and devious, on account no doubt of his having no eyes in the back of his head, and painful too, I fancy, for often he struck against the trunks of trees, or in the tangles of underwood caught his foot, and fell to the ground, flat on his back, or into a great clump of nettles, or of thistles. But still without murmur he came on, until he lay against the fence, with his hands at arm's length grasping the wires. Then he turned, with the intention very likely of going back the way he had come, and I saw his face, and the rest of his front. His face was bloody, his hands also, and thorns were in his scalp.

Alec Reid

From Beginning to Date: Some Thoughts on the Plays of Samuel Beckett

Imagine yourself in Paris on the Left Bank. It is the evening of January 3, 1953, and you are sitting in the tiny Théâtre de Babylone looking at a set depicting a deserted country road. Under a tree a single decrepit figure wearing a bowler hat sits struggling with a boot. The world première of *En Attendant Godot* has just begun, and the play will take about two and a half hours.

Now transport yourself not quite twenty years in time and 3,000 miles in space. You are in New York City in the Lincoln Center. The date is December 7, 1972, and you are sitting in the Repertory Theater. This time there is no scenery, only darkness. Downstage and to your left on an invisible podium stands a tall, motionless figure, faintly lit, shrouded and hooded, sex undeterminable. Its attitude shows that it is gazing intently across stage at a human mouth dimly lit from the front and below, the rest of the face in darkness. The world premiere of *Not I* has just begun, and the play will take about thirteen minutes.

On the January evening in 1953, Beckett did not foresee that *Godot* would be a success; indeed he had prophesied to Roger Blin, his first French director, that given his text and Blin's integrity of acting and direction, *Godot* would play to almost empty houses—probably the best conditions for it. This, however, was the least of his worries; as he was to explain three years later: "Success and failure on the public level never mattered much to me, in fact I feel much more at home with the latter, having breathed deep of its vivifying air all my writing life up to the last couple of years."

Few people would have disputed his forecast. Everything generally accepted as essential to a box-office success is lacking in *Godot*. There is no spectacle, no sex, no violence, hardly any action; as Vivien Mercier penetratingly observed, it is a play where nothing happens, *twice*. There are no fine speeches or brilliant epigrams, only inconsequential exchanges that usually slump into a hopeless silence. For its American premiere in the fashionable Coconut Grove theater in Miami, it had been billed as the laughter sensation of two continents, and who will blame the first-night audience when, as the director, Alan Schneider put it, they left "in droves" long before the interval? Yet this same play has been subsequently performed from Iceland to the Argentine, has been translated into a score of languages, and has been seen by literally millions of people.

This widespread success cannot be explained in the same terms as the success of say *Hamlet* or *My Fair Lady*. Nor can it be a matter of intellectual content since, from the outset, even those who agreed that *Godot* had a "meaning" were deeply divided among themselves as to what that meaning was. One commentator, a devout and sensitive Roman Catholic, saw the play as a statement in dramatic terms of the wretchedness of Man without God, while another, a sensitive and intelligent existentialist, insisted that it is a general expression of the futility of human existence when Man puts his hope in a force outside of himself. Thus Beckett can be presented with equal conviction as a disciple of St. Thomas Aquinas and of Jean-Paul Sartre, while, according to Ruby Cohn, Godot has been variously identified as God, a diminutive god, Love, Death, Silence, Hope, De Gaulle, a Balzac character, a bicycle racer, Time Future, and a Paris street for call girls.

Beckett has steadfastly refused to join in the debate for the very valid reason that he has nothing to add to what he has already written. When Peter Hall, about to direct *Godot* in London, wrote to him seeking an interpretation, Beckett replied that Hall's would be as good as anyone else's. To Alan Schneider, who asked him outright who Godot is or what does Godot mean, Beckett immediately replied with complete candor, "If I knew, I would have said so in the play." During a conversation in 1956, however, he made one very illuminating remark to the effect that the great success of *Waiting for Godot* had arisen from a misunderstanding; critics and public alike, he said, were seeking to impose an allegorical or symbolic explanation on a play which was striving all the time to avoid definition.

From this it follows that if Beckett had achieved his object, the play cannot have any single definitive meaning which would exclude all other meanings. It must be all things to all men, or more accurately, different things to different men. Probably the most valuable description of *Waiting for Godot* appeared in the *San Quentin News*, a paper produced in a California State Penitentiary. Reviewing a presentation of the play in the prison, staff writer C. Bandman writes:

> It was an expression . . . by an author who expects each member of his audience to draw his own conclusions, make his own errors. It asked nothing in point, it forced no dramatized moral on the viewer, it held out no specific hope.

This is true of all Beckett's work for the theater not just of *Godot*. We can get no more and no less from the theatrical experience which Beckett has prepared than we ourselves are ready to put into it. In "Beckett by the Madeleine" (*Columbia University Forum*, Summer 1961), Tom F. Driver takes the point to its logical conclusion: "He [Beckett] has devised his works in such a way that those who comment upon them actually comment upon themselves." Driver goes on to provide a telling example: "One cannot say, 'Beckett has said so and so,' for Beckett has said, 'perhaps'. If the critics and the public see only images of despair, one can only deduce that they are themselves despairing."

While working on this essay, the present writer heard a leading music critic on the radio describe and play the opening of Dvorak's "From the New World," going on to "interpret" it as the composer's memory of his arrival by ship in New York harbor. This "explanation" may help some people to fix the piece in their own experience, but to others it is too personal and too specific. Beckett's plays although using words and therefore in theory being susceptible to verbal paraphrase and analysis, set the same problem; they are like music. As the late George Devine, Beckett's greatest English director, wrote:

> When working as a director on a Beckett play . . . one has to think of the text as something like a musical score, wherein the "notes," the sights, the sounds, the pauses, have their own special inter-related rhythms and out of their composition comes the dramatic impact.

What valid rubric then can the critic find between the extremes of objective, technical description and a subjective account of his own responses?

Fortunately Beckett himself, if all unknowingly, has provided us with considerable help. At the beginning of 1956, he described all his work since World War II as efforts to chart areas of human experience

which the Apollonian artist, eager to achieve some kind of statement, had
hitherto left severely alone. At about the same time, according to Israel
Shenker, Beckett drew an important distinction between his own work
and that of Joyce: "The more Joyce knew, the more he could. He's
tending towards omniscience and omnipotence as an artist. I'm working
with impotence, ignorance." In his letter of August 12, 1957 to Alan
Schneider Beckett wrote:

> I feel the only line is to refuse to be involved in exegesis of any kind. And to
> insist on the extreme simplicity of dramatic situation and issue. . . . we
> have no elucidation to offer of mysteries that are all of their [journalists']
> making. My work is a matter of fundamental sounds (no joke intended)
> made as fully as possible and I accept responsibility for nothing else. If
> people want to have head-aches among the overtones, let them. And provide
> their own aspirin.

The phrase "areas of experience," though convenient, is not wholly
satisfactory, if only because it suggests boundaries, the very act of
definition which Beckett was striving to avoid in *Waiting for Godot*.
More helpful, perhaps, are the words he used over forty years ago in his
monograph on Proust when he speaks of ". . . perilous zones in the life
of the individual dangerous, precarious, painful, mysterious and fertile,
when for a moment the boredom of living is replaced by the suffering of
being." There is nothing paralyzing or deadening about this suffering;
quite the opposite, for as Beckett says, "it is the free play of every
faculty," not simply of the intellect.

Waiting for Godot is an immersion into one such zone of being, the
interplay of ignorance and impotence, but the basic dramatic situation is
simplicity itself. Two friends, Vladimir and Estragon, are waiting to
meet a man called Godot. Although they are not sure what this man looks
like, what they expect from him, or how they came to make the appoint-
ment, they are certain of one thing, that they must keep it. So they go on
waiting until Godot will turn up in person, or, as has always happened in
the past, a messenger arrives from him to say that Godot will not come
that night but will be there the following evening for sure. Until one of
these things happens, Vladimir and Estragon can do nothing. Admittedly
Godot disappointed them the previous night, but who can be sure he will
not come this time? The friends have no means of weighing up the
possibilities, for they know of Godot only what his ambiguous
messenger—or messengers?—can reveal, nor dare they abandon Godot
for they have no means of knowing what this would involve. If they did
so, they would become like Othello, their occupation gone. To stop

waiting would mean a whole new life-style. We, the audience, know from our program that Godot will not come this particular evening, but Vladimir and Estragon have no such certainty and cannot do anything but wait. They do not know and so they cannot do anything but wait. They do not know and so they cannot act; they are ignorant and therefore impotent. Their problem is how to pass the time until the next confrontation perhaps with Godot, perhaps with the messenger. How are they to live through the intervening zone of uncertainty? Originally Beckett thought of calling the play *En Attendant*, and it is in fact about waiting, not about Godot. His sole dramatic function is *not* to come, simply to be waited for. He does not have to exist at all.

Not many of us will have waited, evening after evening, by a tree on a country road for a man who does not come, but again and again in our daily life we find ourselves in situations where we cannot act because we cannot get the knowledge essential to a decision. We have all chafed at the end of a telephone when it seemed the switchboard operator had forgotten us, or raged at an airport over unexplained delays to our plane. "I think," said Beckett in 1956, "anyone nowadays, who pays the slightest attention to his own experience finds it the experience of a non-knower, a non-can-er" (i.e., of someone ignorant, therefore impotent). The worldwide appeal of *Godot* would seem to bear him out. Unfortunately it is the only play of his that most people have heard of, let alone seen, and to know Beckett the dramatist only through *Godot* is as if we knew Shakespeare only through *Romeo and Juliet*.

Nearly four years were to pass between the completion of *Godot* and its first production. Meanwhile Beckett finished the trilogy, paring the novel form down to what even he considered the irreducible minimum and thereby writing himself into a cul-de-sac. In five years he produced only one volume of short prose pieces, but by the end of 1955 he had started once more "struggling with a play." This gave him great difficulty, and not until October 1956 could he report to Schneider that the text was sufficiently definite for him to start work on it with Roger Blin and Jean Martin, the original Pozzo and Lucky: "I am panting to see the realization (i.e. the first run-through on a stage) and know if I am on some kind of road, and can stumble on, or in a swamp." Despite these initial misgivings, *Fin de Partie*, or *Endgame*, was to become Beckett's favorite play.

Like *Godot*, the play is immersion in a zone of being, but in a different one. In the words of the late Jack MacGowran, "If *Godot* is the anguish of waiting, then *Endgame* is the anguish of going." Again the basic dramatic situation is very simple. Hamm, a blind, tyrannical egotist, is slowly dying and to pass the time is trying to complete a long story. Clov, his servant, is bringing himself to leave what they call "the Refuge" and go into a world where all living things are reportedly dead. Nagg and Nell, Hamm's crippled parents, whom he keeps in ash cans, are likewise coming to the end of their days. At the final curtain, Hamm has discarded all the material objects linking him to the world beyond his chair, while Clov, now in traveling clothes, stands beside the door. But we do not know whether he will cross the threshold, in which event Hamm must die, or whether he will remain, preserving for a little longer a status quo that is grinding to a halt.

Inevitably the ash cans attracted wide attention, soon becoming as notorious as Miss Doolittle's famous line in *Pygmalion*, but with more serious consequences. Shaw has not become synonymous with swearing as D. H. Lawrence has with four-letter words, but to the world at large, Beckett is still the dramatist of dustbins, a gloomy, quirky intellectual who could not possibly have anything to offer to the ordinary theatergoer. But taken rightly, those ash cans can provide a key to Beckett's whole dramatic practice and vision. They are themselves, ash cans, nothing more and nothing less; they are not sordid symbols of something else, nor are they scenery merely to illustrate the action; least of all are they comic relief. They are an integral part of the play as the balcony is an integral part of *Romeo and Juliet*, and incidentally they, too, are the setting for an intense and piercingly beautiful love-duet. In the world as we know it we would not expect to find dustbins used as a home for old people, but Beckett is not inviting us to consider the ordinary world. He is presenting us with a microcosm inhabited by people in an extreme situation, the world of Hamm. Hamm can never forgive his parents for having engendered him, but he cannot bring himself to dispose of them finally, just as he cannot bring himself to end his story. Nagg and Nell are legless, cannot move about, so what better place for them than ash cans? When they become obtrusive, they can be kept in their proper place, "bottled" as Hamm puts it, simply by screwing down the lids. When they die, the ash cans can be emptied in the usual manner, by a servant, of course. Given Hamm, this reasoning is logical and true to its context, which is Beckett's sole concern. As he wrote to Alan Schneider: "Hamm as stated and Clov as stated, together as stated, *nec tecum nec sine te*, in such a place and in such a world, that's all I can manage, more than I could."

The Refuge is a hermetically sealed world—"outside of here it's death," as Hamm says—and it provides the prototype for the worlds of *Happy Days*, the mimes, *Play, Breath,* and *Not I*. There can be no traffic between microcosm and macrocosm, unlike the bench in *Come and Go* which serves as a meeting point, and Krapp's den which Fanny, that bony old ghost of a whore, may visit and which Krapp himself may leave for licensed premises or for Evensong. A critic in the London *Times* comparing *Endgame* unfavorably with *Godot*, complained that while Vladimir and Estragon were human, "the creatures in this play belong to the private world of Mr. Samuel Beckett's imaginings." To a point he is quite right. Beckett himself has described *Endgame* as less human than *Godot*, and the people in the Refuge do belong to the world of Beckett's imaginings. But this is no longer a private world; Beckett has laid it in front of us and we, should we wish, can enter it, often finding to our surprise that we are learning more about our own private microcosm. A few days before his death, George Devine recalled his first meeting with Beckett: "This man seemed to have lived and suffered so that I might see, and he was generous enough to pass it on to me."

The "realization" of *Fin de Partie* assured Beckett that he was now out of the swamp and on a road, that by returning to the theater he had escaped from the impasses to which the trilogy had led him. Significantly, because contrary to his custom he has dedicated the play—to Roger Blin. A period of intense creativity followed; within thirty months Beckett had finished two radio plays, two mimes, and the monologue *Krapp's Last Tape*. He had also begun to compose in English again, something he had not done for nearly fifteen years.

The two *Actes sans paroles* are not mimes in the usually accepted sense of the evocation through gesture and expression of an imagined character in an imagined situation. Rather they are plays with the character and the situation present before our eyes. Beckett has set down a sequence of stage directions with no intervening speeches, acts without words. Both pieces are about Man and those external forces which he cannot control. The first mime falls within the zone of ignorance-impotence, while the second is a translation into visible movements of a pattern which itself expresses an idea. They are effective stage pieces, but by definition they lack one element essential in Devine's list of what goes to make the full dramatic impact of a Beckett play. Since they have no words, there can be no pauses and no interrelated rhythms of sound and silence.

The broadcast plays have had a profound influence on Beckett's stage work, both directly and indirectly. The obvious and immediate example is *Krapp's Last Tape*. Through his work on *All That Fall*, Beckett had become a practitioner in disembodied sound and had acquired some direct experience with the mechanics of sound recording. On December 14, 1957, Beckett heard the Irish actor, Patrick Magee, who had played Slocum in *All That Fall*, reading Beckett's *From an Abandoned Work* on the BBC, Third Programme. In less than two months, Beckett had finished the first draft of what he called *The Magee Monologue* which, renamed *Krapp's Last Tape*, was first staged in London on October 28, 1958. Beckett tells us on the program that the play is set in the future, thereby overcoming the problem of how Krapp-at-39 could have been using a machine not then invented. Technically *Krapp's Last Tape* is a monologue in that it uses only one actor, but in fact it is a confrontation between Krapp-at-69 and Krapp-at-39. The voice on the tape is as much a *dramatis persona* as the old man we see pottering about on the stage in front of us. But it is essential that we *see* him as well as hear him. Like *Under Milk Wood, Krapp's Last Tape* is a play for voices, but not disembodied voices.

Again the basic dramatic situation is very simple. Krapp on his sixty-ninth birthday plays a tape made thirty years previously and is brought face to face with the failure of his life. Like a soul in purgatory, he relives the moment of his greatest transgression, the rejection of life. Here we see in action the anguish of heightened awareness, another zone of being in which much is suffered but about which nothing can validly be said. The play is not about something, it is that thing itself.

Apart from *Godot*, no play of Beckett's has provoked wider extremes of "interpretation" than his next piece, *Happy Days*. A learned American professor has called it Beckett's ambiguous celebration of human persistence, while a distinguished French actress describes it as a marvellous love poem, the song of a woman who still wants to see and hear the man she loves. Looking at it another way, we can see it as an amalgam of *Godot* and *Endgame*. At first sight the dramatic situation looks like a variation of that in *Godot*. Winnie, caught in steadily deteriorating circumstances from which she cannot escape and in which she must draw increasingly on her inner resources, has to pass the time between the bell for waking and the bell for sleeping. But here, it might seem, Godot appears. Willie, Winnie's husband, for some time out of sight but never out of mind, comes to visit her from his hole on the other side of the mound which is engulfing her. The purpose of his visit, however, is ambiguous, and we never know what happens any more than we know whether Clov crosses the threshold of the Refuge. Our guess —for it can be no more than that—will largely determine how we view the play and will expose us as romantics or cynics, optimists or defeatists. *Happy Days* goes much farther than *Godot*; it is not simply a study in survival, but of survival on the very edge of nothing.

At this point convenience suggests we depart from strict chronological sequence and consider two short pieces, *Come and go*, (1965) and *Breath* (1966). Presented consecutively as a double bill, they would take up roughly six minutes of running time. Like *Acte sans paroles 11*, and the film which Beckett made in 1964, *Come and Go* is a highly successful attempt to translate into visible terms what might be called the shape of an idea. *Breath* has no words, no actors, no sequence of events or time, no specified place, but is only a combination of sound and light increasing and diminishing. It raises the basic question of what is a theatrical experience, a question that can only be answered in the theater itself. In *Play*, his next major dramatic work, Beckett abandons every suggestion of naturalism in the sights and sounds which he presents to his audience. The stage is dimly lit, but we can just see three urns with a human head protruding from each. As the play proceeds, a beam of light situated between actors and audience is constantly jabbing at the heads, revealing faces "so lost to age and aspect," to quote Beckett's directions, "as to seem part of the urns." These *dramatis personae* have no names but are referred to on the program as First Woman, Man, and Second Woman. The dramatic situation based on an eternal triangle requires that we should know the sex of the participants, but their bodies are irrelevant and hence contained in the urns. Their faces are expressionless, their voices toneless except for the five occasions where the text gives a definite instruction. The specific has been reduced to a minimum; here is no microcosm but as near infinity and eternity as Beckett can bring us.

Our first reaction is of irritated bewilderment at what we see, and incomprehension of what we hear. The actors are constantly interrupted by the light eliciting speech or imposing silence. Gradually the inklings of a story emerge, the hint of an eternal triangle, but there is nothing definite, no explanation of the urns or of the light. We are precisely in the situation of the trio on the stage; for us, as for them, past experience seems irrelevant and the present is meaningless. We begin to sympathize with them. Then, without any break or warning, *Play* is repeated exactly. The two women and the man know only what they did when the curtain rose for the first time, but we, in the light of the knowledge we have gained, now understand their situation and their sufferings more clearly every minute. Increased understanding brings us heightened awareness, and we move deeper and deeper into the play. As we do so, we suffer more because we have become more closely identified with the protagonists. Spectator has become sharer, and a third run-through would be intolerable.

Watching *Godot* we find parallels in our own experience for the anguish of Vladimir and Estragon waiting in ignorance and impotence, but in *Play* the impact works differently and more directly. Here we are not watching Beckett as he explores a zone of being, we are plunged into that zone ourselves. During the second run-through, we are much in the position of Krapp-at-69 as he listens to the tape of Krapp-at-39. Beckett achieves this impact by the simple though brilliantly original process of repeating the play. The words themselves remain exactly the same; it is we who change. As the Irish poet Bryan Guinnes has said, great art is that magic which enables us to see with another man's eyes, feel with another man's heart, without recourse to the roundabout method of description.

Yet amazingly many people have found it possible to write about *Play* and "interpret" it without so much as mentioning the repetition.

So to *Not I*, the latest and most concentrated of Beckett's works for the stage. All that one can profitably say of it is that it is pure theater, which can exist and be experienced only in an auditorium. It is itself and nothing else; trying to describe it or its impact in words is like trying to describe in words the impact of a glass of pure water. Throughout his artistic life, Beckett has been striving to say the unsayable, and he now confronts the critic with the same task.

In *Not I* there is a silent, hooded figure, immobile save for four small gestures of the arms; there is a disembodied mouth, with lips, tongue, jaws, working frenziedly throughout; there is a voice, impersonal, limpid, beautifully articulating, which fills the auditorium with broken, almost incoherent phrases in telegraphese; there is an incredible story about a miracle—speech and feeling suddenly regained by an old woman after sixty years. All this can be said, and it amounts to nothing; yet I, for one, left the theater knowing that for thirteen minutes I had been living at full stretch with mind, heart, and physical senses working all out. By a process similar to that in *Play*, I had been immersed in one of those zones where for a brief instant the boredom of living is replaced by the suffering of being. I had known all the anguish of the inability to understand. "Scoured" was the first word I used to describe the experience; "purged" would have been Aristotle's.

In this little canter through the plays, we have been striving all the time to avoid attributing to Beckett philosophies and ideas that were never his but our own. We have likewise tried to keep clear of "interpretations" if only because there can be no definitive ones. If Beckett's plays are to mean anything to us, we must translate them into our own terms and understand them from our own experiences. Their strength lies not in what they say to the world at large (which is very little) but in what they do to each one of us in the audience. Herein lies their novelty and their challenge.

George Devine's program note to *Play* begins:

> When we first see a new kind of painting or listen to a new kind of music, we realize that we have to make an adjustment in ourselves and our attitude if we are to get the best out of the experience. So it is with the plays of Samuel Beckett.

With luck, these observations will make that readjustment a little easier, not through what they argue (which is very little) but through what they may provoke.

Jan Hokenson

Three Novels in Large Black Pauses

After completing the stories, still writing in French, still working in the first person for his fiction, Beckett wrote the trilogy of novels that many readers consider his finest work: *Molloy, Malone Dies*, and *The Unnamable*. Not only the pinnacle of Beckett's narrative canon, the trilogy is often considered one of the masterworks of western literature. More than a prismatic portrait of the modern writer struggling for self-expression, the trilogy is a profound testament to human anguish, impotence, and courageous humor in a moribund world. In the trilogy, Beckett addresses the paramount concerns of modern man and modern art: the fictivity of all human expression, the corrosion of the western cultural heritage, the craving for knowledge and for love in a cold irrational universe, the frailty of "I" in the clamor of perceptions and the chaos of experience. But with consummate artistry, Beckett turns such abstractions into concrete experiences.

The trilogy begins in tones and motifs familiar from *Texts for Nothing*—the derelict exile, the quest, the paralysis, a voice buzzing in an ear. But the emphasis is new, for the world of the trilogy is unlike any other in Beckett's work. It is a world in dissolution, in which shapes, concepts, and the most rudimentary certainties dissolve as the narrators atrophy. "I listen," says Molloy, "and the voice is of a world collapsing endlessly."

From volume to volume of the trilogy, Beckett maps a world mysteriously subject to endless collapse. Few people or objects remain whole, upright, or mobile for long. Tires go flat, key rings break, lights go out, sounds cease. Intuited notions break down almost as rapidly as concepts, disintegrating into fragments, incoherent or inapplicable. Ideation becomes laughable, memories fluid, and perceptions unreliable, until very little remains accessible to expression.

"Is there any reason," Beckett asked in a letter to a painter friend, Axel Kaun, "why that terribly arbitrary materiality of the world's surface should not be dissolved, as, for example, the tonal surface, eaten into by large black pauses, in Beethoven's Seventh Symphony, so that for pages at a time we cannot perceive it other than, let us say, as a vertiginous path of sounds connecting unfathomable abysses of silence?" Beckett's question implies that materiality is mere sheathing over something else, and he asks whether it is possible to dissolve the world's surface, so as to reveal the immaterial.

In the trilogy, body precipitates into tongue, mind precipitates into a sensibility, expression precipitates into words. The residuum in the last volume is an appalling realm wherein the words almost cease to mean, and discourse itself dissolves in negations through which nothingness surges up to become perceptible.

Beckett charts a vertiginous path through a world in dissolution, menaced by mysterious collapse and ringed with chasms of silence. There is no causal premise for such dissolution, and there is nothing with which to combat it, nothing but "the old thoughts . . . shreds of old visions," and the courage of irrepressible humor.

Nor is it the kind of dissolution to which we are accustomed in literary worlds—structures cracking in Shakespearean storms, noses falling off the faces of Gogol's grotesques. Where materiality is arbitrary, dissolution is more than a stylistic technique or a symbolic device. The reader of the trilogy, who is willing to read through the dissolution of world, body, and language, will read into the large black pauses that have appalled and dismayed some listeners of Beethoven.

I "THE THING IN RUINS"

The trilogy opens onto "frozen wastes" and "muddy solitudes." Urban or rural, the terrain is potholed, tripping upright man to his knees. The landscape is parceled out in units of devastation, garbage dumps and deadening gardens, ditches, and blind alleys, tyrannized pantry or parish, sucking bogs and menacing forests. Slinking through the dank byways of a moribund world, Beckett's monologuists lose the locomotive aids of bicycle, crutches, or stick, and they can scarcely haul the human carcass forward; they end in a bed or a room where they write, destitute and alone.

When Beckett turned from English to French, he turned away from more than a language. Abandoning the third person, he abandoned the pretext of a stable exterior perspective, investing the narrative in "I," and forcing the reader to enter that vast and protean realm of man alone. "[I] in all that inner space one never sees, the brain and heart and other caverns where thought and feeling dance their sabbath." It is at once an Irish jig and a *danse macabre*.

The comic and confidently brilliant intellection of *Murphy* and *Watt* cedes, in French, to the awful ruins of philosophic meditation and religious sensibility. Only pointed vulgarity and bitter irony accompany the dissolution of world and self into "muddy solitudes." The lives of the trilogy's monologuists are over. Alone without god or fellowman, with only the "craving for a fellow" and the "brave company" of a few cherished objects transported from the world to a womblike shelter where the writers write, they try to explain past experience but can make no sense of it.

Not for want of training. Beckett makes it clear that in the dim past his narrators suffered the best of classical educations. In their diffident allusions, they exhibit a close acquaintance with philosophy, theology, arts, mathematics, and sundry other analytic and creative disciplines. Unusually intelligent, Beckett's monologuists are unusually well versed in the western cultural heritage. But like the bodies rotting away, the heritage does not serve. In a world collapsing endlessly, the long rich tapestry of western traditions unravels to "shreds of old visions." Thus, received ideas come in scraps, half-concepts, and half-quotations which never cohere into a useful and intelligible whole.

Moran's bourgeois life is a sham, from paternal devotion to communion, but he learns disgust with it, concluding, crippled, "I am ready to leave it all." His allusions to religion and philosophy, in particular, are bewildered when not bitter. For these two forms of thought most overtly promise redemption, and from volume to volume Beckett shreds received ideas of religion and philosophy, excoriating them as false promises and useless abstractions in a world of concrete problems without solution. In a world dissolving materially, collapsing intellectually, promises of salvation are at best impertinent, at worst cruel and obscene.

Unquestioning faith in a lie is worse than the lie itself. To fugitive Molloy, "morning is the time to hide. They wake up hale and hearty, their tongues hanging out for order, beauty and justice, baying for their due." He who questions is alone, a derelict exile or mercifully delivered into a shelter to testify to inexplicable decay and his own perplexity. Molloy muses on his "rags" of astronomy, geology, anthropology, psychiatry, but "my knowledge of men was scant and the meaning of

being beyond me. Oh I've tried everything. In the end it was magic that had the honour of my ruins. . . . And the thing in ruins, I don't know what it is."
    Neither does Beckett. For centuries we have called it "I." In the first volume of the trilogy, Beckett's "I" is a "thing in ruins," beholding ruins, trying but unable to make sense of experience. Single events are clear, but their sources and interrelationships are mysterious. World is as enigmatic as mind, and even in the first volume they seem to diminish together.

II "CHRIST, THERE'S CRAWLING"

    Two travel tales comprise *Molloy*, a novel whose halves sometimes seem like oddly refracted mirror images of each other. Alone, each narrative would make an excellent short story, peculiar but not profoundly disturbing—Molloy's a rather shambling digressive meditation on a journey, Moran's a rather fastidious bungled detective story. It is together, as Beckett wrote them, that the two narratives resonate with mysterious echoes and modulations of each other, elaborating a labyrinthine whole far greater than its two parts.
    Writing in his mother's bed, Molloy describes "the unreal journey" of his search; noting that he is beginning to resemble her more and more, he describes how, traveling in the only region he has ever known, he was continually lost and never found her. In turn, Moran reports his search for Molloy, whom he never found but came to resemble. The first sought his mother, and the second, with his son, sought the first.
    On that level of description, *Molloy* seems a parable about two searchers assimilated by the object of their quest. For they began as quite different men, Molloy the derelict sceptic and Moran the landed bourgeois. Yet the changes that they undergo in body, temperament, and even prose, the encounters and events on their respective journeys, even the scenery—several aspects of their quests share a strange resemblance. Both men remark, for instance, on their stiffening legs and missing teeth, their inability to distinguish blue and green, their low-hanging testicles, their joy at the prospect of complete physical immobility; they both ride and then abandon bicycles, meet shepherds tending black sheep, murder men who resemble them, feel kindly toward men carrying sticks . . . and so on. Every reader tracks parallels and casts about for explanations, often turning to theoretical schemes and mythic-heroic prototypes.
    Events in *Molloy*, springing from mysterious causes and interacting in mysterious ways, seem like part of a vast over arching cipher. Thence a

mythic dimension, which Beckett nourishes with shreds of old legends, fables, and parables, Homer's *Odyssey*, Dante's *Divine Comedy*, the Christian Passion, and Bunyan's *Pilgrim's Progress*. But in the world of *Molloy*, the shining legends shrivel into sour parody. Molloy's Circe is the mannish Lousse gardening her magic realm, his Nausicaa appears to him on a garbage heap, his Cyclops is a red-pawed policeman. At times we infer ironic parallels with legendary voyagers, and at other times the monologuist makes the comparison himself. Molloy's journey seems to him "a veritable Calvary with no limits to its stations and no hope of crucifixion." During this Calvary, Molloy displays the bravery of suffering heroes and the wile of fabulous voyagers. When reduced to near paralysis, he exclaims, "Christ, there's crawling," and grapples on.

His journey ends in further loss and redoubled mystery. Molloy never does know why he decided to seek his mother, why he missed his goal but arrived in her room, why he is ordered to report the journey for the Sunday visitor. Moran does not know why *his* Sunday visitor orders him after Molloy, why he seems to know about Molloy but has never met him, why he is ordered back before finding his quarry, why the voice tells him to write the report.

Conjecturing endlessly, they find no answers to their questions. Nor do we. We can maneuver mock-heroic scenes and allusions into parodic analogy, but we learn very little from that about the relentless decay of these searchers and their world. Questioning as doggedly as Oedipus, in a no less putrescent and dissolute world, they never discover the secret sin or original cause that brought them to such a pass. Instead things wind down in lockstep; Molloy's decay is echoed in Moran's decay, the second narrative enshadows the first, mystery explicates mystery, and the novel becomes a case of *obscurum per obscuriora*: the resolution is even more perplexing than the problem.

The detective story is, at root, a quest for truth in a sordid world teeming with suspicious characters, implausible motives, and red herrings. The detective is a questioner whose superior brain solves the puzzle and assigns the guilt. Beckett sardonically uses that atmosphere and that expectation in setting Moran off in quest of Molloy.

It may be that in Sophoclean fashion Moran is his own quarry, or it may be that the answers matter less than the nature of the questions. Increasingly Moran questions the surface structure of his own existence, his materialistic penchant for house and garden, his religiosity and the perhaps imaginary status of his chief, Youdi, and so on; at the end of his devastating journey he is expectedly "dispossessed of self" but enjoys "a sharper sense of identity." Yet all he has accomplished is to have decayed physically and left his household to moulder, to have lost his quarry and nearly every possession, to have moved from unquestioning faith to questionnaires and proliferating unknowns, and to have redundantly announced that neither his body nor his language are those of the old Moran.

Negatives all. As the second half closes the circle, we are left spinning in redoubled obscurities. Moran has no answers to his questionnaire, nor can he explain his own positive valuation of his own decay. All we know is that he has moved from one circumstance and manner of thinking to another, indeed from Moran's to Molloy's. Devastation of material world and body reveals a more essential core, which Moran values but cannot explain. But having finished his report on mysterious events for an unknown master, Moran is ready to swing off on his new crutches again after Molloy; so the rounding on the circular cipher of journeys begins again.

III   *"MY LITTLE PENCIL DWINDLES"*

Malone undermines the relative certainties of *Molloy*. Not knowing how he arrived in his room, Malone vaguely remembers a forest. He amuses himself "with trying to invent them, those same lost events. But without succeeding in amusing myself really." This dying writer is finished with events and will tell himself a different kind of story. And Beckett hurls the reader, as though down a circle of Dante's hell, from perplexities and pains to still greater pain and corrosion.

Malone awaits death, the last physical dissolution. He has never lived properly, he thinks; always too earnestly grave and questioning. Now he is through with living, questioning, and earnestness. He will play, passing the time while dying with stories, so that we witness his creation of characters. But he does not succeed in amusing himself. His story becomes a most earnest affair. And life intrudes on him in the person of his mysterious visitor, for whom he formulates, of all things, a questionnaire. He writes not three stories, but only one, and that one remains unfinished when death apparently overtakes him.

Malone is unable to carry out a single intention. A goal that he misses is stasis. "I shall be neutral and inert," he begins. But he often panics, in dread of events or throes of death. For stasis is impossible. *Molloy's* duality as two stories has become a duality of creator and story, but the same unrelenting process of parallel destitution obtains. Even as he decomposes, Malone composes a story that almost caricatures *Molloy*, as bourgeois Sapo transforms into derelict Macmann. Far from neutral, the creator gradually infuses himself into his creation, ending with "a little creature in my image" who, when Malone loses his possessions, loses *his* possessions. The two orders of life, real and fictional, resonate with echoes and modulations of each other, splitting the novel into mirror images of "I," diminishing together.

Even death is not a stasis, but a whelping, not a terminus but a birth. As it was to Molloy and Moran, life is a long inexplicable decay, a rotting away from the bone and brain. Such cursed living seems to have something penitential about it, but, unable to assign cause, Malone simply awaits release: birth, mercifully, into an existence as black silent nothing. Anticipating the moment of release, Malone feels like "an old foetus."

Fulcrumlike at the trilogy's midpoint, Malone balances between two orders of existence. His dying resonates both backward to the gradual paralyses of Molloy and Moran, and forward to the utter dissolution of the Unnamable. But Malone's dying is also a tenuous balance between fact and fiction, body and mind, material life and imaginative life.

In the same exercise book with the same pencil, as he points out, Malone writes about the events that befall both himself and his character. The division is at first neat, in distinct prose styles and tenses. And matters are at first so simple, even "little events" so scant, that Malone's project seems certain of success: "present state, three stories, inventory, there." He composes his "present state" as planned, but not too satisfactorily, for it clarifies little and consists half in questions that he cannot answer. He at once embarks on his story and the balance of his plan.

It goes badly awry, for Malone is *dying*. It may be that death is a birth into another state, but it is certain that death is a dying from life, and Malone finds that process horrible. Eyes dim, speech gurgles, hearing fades, neck stiffens, and movement resides in fingers and eyelids only. Through over half his time, Malone is served food and slops; then they too cease. No less than his own solid flesh, the material surface of his world begins to defy the observing intelligence: walls shimmer, floors whiten, the room pulsates. When Malone loses his stick, he loses all his material possessions in an instant. Loss compounds loss, in body as in world.

But Malone's fingers scribble on across his page, reporting these events and delineating his character. He begins Sapo in a fictional world of such unimpeachable stability, solidity, and banality, that the boy himself is soon bored. Parodying realistic style, Malone takes his hero from the Saposcats' healthy world to the Lamberts' world of incest and slaughter. There the Molloyesque disequilibrium begins, as lentils do not stack, mules succumb sideways, hens teeter on one leg, and the hero himself develops a stumbling, wavering walk.

Dying, Malone creates "my other," "another whose life is just beginning." The career of Malone's vice-exister encapsulates the mortal course from youth to helpless age and destitution. Old Sapo on the bench is soon renamed Macmann, as his author sardonically mocks both theological and aesthetic ideas of life and creation. The creator implants his new "son of man" in an absurd world, known as the House of Saint John of God. The inmates make no sense of anything to anyone and the regulations are unknown or incomprehensible, just as in Malone's own abode. Love is even more comically grotesque than with Molloy's maiden of offal—or with the real couple writhing in Malone's sight. Lemuel batters himself and bangs Macmann on the head—just as the funereal visitor bangs on Malone's own skull.

As the reader tracked parallels in the careers of Molloy and Moran, he now tracks parallels in Malone's real and fictional worlds. They are similarly interdependent, and they end together, in deliberate "mixture of Macmann and agony."

Gradually, the tension between fact and fiction disorders fundamental certainties about the "real." Which is more real to Malone, the material existence in the realm of pots, or the immaterial existence in imagination? Malone exists in both, recording them on the same page and soon failing to distinguish them by paragraph or even tense. His fictional mad Saxon flees the material world "aghast at such depths of opacity." Malone himself wonders whether his own world with its walls and floors is not nonexistent, whether he is really alive or already dead and "in reality all that is perhaps nothing but my worms." Questioning the substantiality of objects, even as he invents others for his story, Malone subjects the "real" to both destruction and creation. Meanwhile the one object remaining to him, his little pencil, dwindles as it writes, diminishing as implacably as creator and character.

Malone Dies brings the trilogy to midpoint in several ways, developing the motifs but changing the focus. Even as the material world begins to moulder and fade, we watch an immaterial world unfold in the mind of a dying man. He recreates himself in fiction, delineating an avatar of "the child I might have been, why not," then of the inmate he seems to be. For although he at first tries to tell a different kind of story, Malone learns that he can create only fictional images of himself. Relentless decay pervades both orders of existence, and in "the crumbling away of two little heaps," creator and character exhibit the entropic condition of mortality. As death overtakes Malone, corpses proliferate in his story. As his light dims, lights blaze in his story. As he gasps, he pleads that death will cease in his story. But fiction cannot save him, and his life seems to disintegrate utterly in his crumbling syntax, then silence.

In body as in mind, Malone was a thing in ruins, "talking of myself, my mind wandering, far from here, among its ruins." His life seemed an irrational riddle, and intellection thus a horrendous impertinence. But with the writer's ability to create fictional life, for "brave company" and possibly even love, Malone combatted the dissolution of one world with the creation of another. Then both worlds are superseded by a third, the strange realm of an unnamable entity who does not know whether he is being or nothingness, fact or fiction, material or even extant.

IV "A DEAD TONGUE"

Moving from Malone's deathbed to a still more problematical level of discourse, Beckett invests the last narrative in a creature who knows neither who, what, nor where he is. In his "preamble" he tries to situate himself in space and time, but he cannot. Space consists in infinite reaches of gray in which lights occasionally gleam and the lifeless form of Malone orbits round him; his world seems to be a boundless void but, unable to touch or even to prod the darkness with a stick, he is unable to define a relationship to anything. His memories blur, and present events—gleaming lights and stifled cries—occur eratically, depriving him of the ability to gauge his existence in time.

Like Malone he is a maker of fictions, and he has created numerous fictional existences for himself—notably the lives of every narrative hero in Beckett's canon "from Murphy onwards"—now including even "Malone, from whom nothing further is to be hoped." Through those fictions, which he sneeringly dismisses as fables and fairy tales, he sought to enlist sufferers of his pains. But he has never succeeded, really, in creating surrogates to suffer and exist for him; so now he hopes to foreswear fiction and speak at last of himself.

It is an appalling enterprise, for he is unable to verify a single aspect of his own nature, and he feels like an alien thing in the modes of self-expression. Every affirmation becomes conjecture, question, finally denial—then, hastily, another hypothesis to keep the quest going. It is an endless churn of questions, because the materiality of both world and self has dissolved, and existence in Beckett's unfathomable abysses of silence is not susceptible to proof.

By dint of scrupulous inquiry, the last monologuist at first determines that he is endowed with sight, hearing, and touch. He seems to possess a body, and ongoing organic processes would seem to be confirmed by the sensation of falling tears, though they may be liquified brain. He eventually denies having an ear, a mouth, a neck, and so on.

Even with respect to his own materiality, inquiry ends in denial, and he concludes that "only I and this black void have ever been."

Discarnate in a darkness, what is he? If existence is not material, what is it? He renounces the status of word-user, that primal human distinction. He contends that his true self has never been expressed in all his words hitherto, and that he has succeeded only in "bungling" himself in all his attempts at verbal self-expression.

But just as the splendid imagination of Malone was fastened to a dying body, so this unnamable entity is fastened to a speaking voice. Malone watched his hands curl on the bed sheet like alien objects, and the Unnamable hears his voice chatter like a distant creek, spilling words that bear no relation to him. It is "a dead tongue" foisted on the living, and it is as confining and inescapable as Malone's body.

Language assumes a terrible materiality to this bodiless being who has no other locus of existence. Words are so alien that they seem like objects floating in space, or flakes falling in this void. For centuries man has defined himself through abstract systems expressed in words, and the living entity that would define himself without them is plunged into a darkness swirling with syllogisms and the parts of speech.

Most damnable are the pronouns, and "I" the reddest herring of all. Beckett's sustained duality now widens into the chasm between "I" and "not I." Heroically as he tries, with each stratagem more clever than the last, the Unnamable is unable to avoid "I"—that pronoun so august and privileged since the Renaissance. Battering language with ingenious ploys and serpentine maneuvers, the Unnamable concludes as he began, "I, say I. Unbelieving."

He knows, dimly, who he is, "he who I know I am." But confined to language, the only knowledge that he can receive and convey is that gained through words. Through his fictions and the tyrannical voice, he has learned all the lessons that pupils of life and death are taught. "No denying it," he says, "I'm confoundedly well-informed," then promptly adds, "No good wriggling, I'm a mine of useless knowledge." For all his pains, the intellectual heritage has informed him only of its own emptiness, its utter irrelevance to elemental being. It is possible that there is one lesson that he has forgotten, for he does not understand the first thing about life and death, yet he seems condemned to exist stupidly, in the penitential fashion, in this black limbo between them. If the trivial teachings of a tattered heritage can save him, it must, logically, be through some obscure lesson that he has forgotten how to recite.

But the Unnamable finds this notion of a forgotten pensum feeble, and he soon moves on to consider other alternatives. His existence is a curse with only one possible salvation; perhaps the proper chance combination of words will somehow name him. But in a world that has dissolved, language is a closed system, and words refer only to each other.

In such a dilemma, rational man would give up. Beckett's Unnamable, however, is not merely a rational intelligence locked up in an absurd world but also an elemental being, nonconceptual and nonverbal. Since his first "vice-existence" as Murphy, he has mocked the poor resources of reason and consciously fled to the alienation of the mad. But Murphy's and even Watt's subversive intellection withered on the threshold of the trilogy, where Beckett no longer uses mind to combat the abuses of mind. Molloy apprehended experience through darkly seen images sketched with loathing, and the first volume of the trilogy inaugurated a progression in alogically imaginative, imaged prose. Malone lived and died in his exercise book, mingling himself and his imaginative fiction. The Unnamable has tried to dispense with images, approximations, tropes, fictions, the subtlest analogies that bedevil our speech, and to state exactly who he is.

The task of defining ·and naming nonverbal being seems hopeless. Perched somewhere in a darkness over an abyss into which falling things vanish, the Unnamable soon exhausts, chestnut by chestnut, combinations and even topics of conversation. He turns to the resorts of fable, at first laconically to keep the words gurgling and the alternatives open, then passionately when he decides that finding his *own* story is his sole recourse.

The advantage of story is that it posits an existence which one can believe, and, with a bit of effort, wriggle into, thus breaking free of limbo. The disadvantage is that story is verbal and that language itself is a symbolic structure in which the word "chair" has as little to do with that object as the word "I" has to do with the self. The only way to reconcile those circumstances is to *become* a verbal character, an "I."

It is an abortive effort, like its predecessors. Living being can no more assume verbal existence than a bench can become its noun. The Mahood stories are comic failures, blatant impossibilities. Abandoning the hopeless effort to become an "I," the Unnamable spurns human existence and decides to create an elemental nonhuman existence, Worm. But he might just as well have created "chair." Without language, the creation can neither communicate with nor receive the communications of the creator. The Unnamable is forced to endow Worm with an ear, that vehicle of language, so as to plunge his creation into a "hellish repertory" of mere words.

In a black void the words soon churn in frenzy. The rhythm of panic is haunting, for it conveys the vibrant essence of this living being without naming it. Layer by layer, the world of the trilogy has tunneled from the surface to this dark abyss of silence roofed with words. The relationship of language to essential being is expressible only in words, and it can therefore never be known. Volume by volume, the surface materiality of world and self has dissolved into sounds and silence, or large black pauses beneath words. In the pauses— technically, the interstices—the reader must imagine.

Like the Unnamable, he has no other choice. The trilogy is a verbal work of art, struggling against language but confined to print. That the distillation of self from world, imagination from body, being from language, occurs in words, is one of Beckett's most astounding achievements. In words, Beckett affirms existence that is neither material nor verbal. After world, body, and even language dissolve, there remains being, undefined and unnamed but manifestly present in anguished rhythms, bitter comic tones, and sheer unending will to be.

Hersh Zeifman

Religious Imagery in the Plays of Samuel Beckett

In Samuel Beckett's early poem "Enueg I," there is a passage which reads: "at Parnell Bridge a dying barge carrying a cargo of nails and timber rocks itself softly in the foaming cloister of the lock." Of it Martin Esslin has written: "We were in a broadcasting studio preparing a reading of the poem in Beckett's presence. At this point [the lines cited above] he asked the reader to put a little more stress on the nails and timber, which, after all, stood for the cross. So intimately is the descriptive linked to the symbolic in these poems!" Esslin's comment is apt, although it applies not only to the poems, so intimately is the descriptive linked to the symbolic in all of Beckett's work. And to a major extent, the symbolic in Beckett's work means the religiously symbolic. Often the symbols are explicit; even the most casual reader cannot help but be aware that Beckett's writings are packed with direct Biblical quotation and theological terms. But just as often they are implicit, gaining in weight of religious reference by means of context and juxtaposition, echo and reverberation.

In the above-quoted lines of poetry, we have Beckett's own testimony that "nails and timber" was intended to convey an implicit religious image, an image repeated in slightly expanded form in his novel *Molloy*: "It was a cargo of nails and timber, on its way to some carpenter I suppose" (Christ, of course, earned his living as a carpenter). Even without such testimony, however, the perceptive reader should have grasped the underlying religious implications of the image, for it fits quite naturally into a familiar context, namely Beckett's constant allusions to the death of Christ generally (note that the barge is "dying") and to the

Crucifixion specifically (the "timber" links up with Beckett's frequent use of the Biblical identification of cross with tree; the "nails" is self-explanatory). It is precisely in its skilfully woven pattern of implicit religious imagery that so much of the textural richness of Beckett's work resides. And it is particularly in his plays, in which the continuously present visual element necessarily adds an extra dimension to the merely verbal, that this underlying pattern becomes most apparent, a pattern embodying the basic metaphysical and theological issues at the heart of all Beckett's work: suffering, death, guilt, judgment, and salvation.

The suffering that characterizes earthly existence and the theological context of that suffering are recurrent leitmotivs in Beckett's drama. The casual relationship between divine cruelty and human suffering is perhaps most effectively dramatized in Beckett's portrayal of many of his characters as emblematic Biblical sufferers. In this way, Beckett implies that, like the Biblical figures with whom they are consistently assimilated, his characters suffer as a consequence of divine punishment. And the Biblical sufferer with whom Beckett's characters are most frequently identified is Christ, whose death on the cross is, for Beckett, a paradigm of divine rejection. Occasionally, the comparison is explicit; thus, in *Waiting for Godot*, Estragon admits, "All my life I've compared myself to [Christ]". More often, however, it is implicit; in order to grasp the underlying religious connotation, one must first pay careful attention to all the elements of Beckett's dramaturgy, verbal and nonverbal alike.

In *Endgame*, for example, the wretchedness of life, immediately placed in a theological context by means of an implicit link with the Crucifixion, is suggestively planted in the play's opening moments —even before the characters have an opportunity to *tell* us of their wretchedness. The first thing we notice is the set with its death images. Thus the picture with its face to the wall evokes a mood of mourning; in orthodox Judaism, for instance, it is the custom to turn pictures to the wall in the home of someone who has recently died. The two sheets covering Hamm and his parents are likewise death images, recalling the shrouds used to cover corpses. And the two ash cans or dustbins, containing the decaying flesh of Nagg and Nell, are linked with the grave via such religious images as "earth to earth, ashes to ashes, dust to dust." But we also notice that the set itself resembles a skull, with its "*bare interior,*" two small windows reminiscent of eye sockets and what we later discover are hollow walls: "Do you hear? ([*Hamm*] *strikes the wall with his knuckles.*) Do you hear? Hollow bricks! (*He strikes again.*) All that's hollow!" The symbolism of a skull-like set is significant when we recall that Christ was crucified at Golgotha, "that is to say, a place of a skull" (*Matthew* 27:33).

This visual link with the crucified Christ is extended when Clov begins to speak, for the first words he utters are, "Finished, it's finished . . . ," the words spoken by Christ on the cross. And Hamm's first speech contains the lament, "Can there be misery . . . loftier than mine?" linking him not only with Jeremiah, who cried, "Behold, and see if there be any sorrow like unto my sorrow, which is done unto me, wherewith the Lord hath afflicted me in the day of his fierce anger" (*Lamentations* 1:12), but also, more significantly, with the Christ of Herbert's poem "The Sacrifice," with its repeated lament, "Was ever grief like mine?" In addition, Hamm has a blood-stained handkerchief over his face, calling to mind the legend of Saint Veronica, a legend previously alluded to by Beckett in the poem "Enueg II": "veronica mundi / veronica munda / give us a wipe for the love of Jesus." And, as many critics have noted, both Hamm and Clov carry echoes of the Crucifixion in their very names (Hamm—*hamm*er, and also *hamus*, Latin for "hook"; Clov—*clou*, French for "nail").

Because Beckett's characters suffer so intensely, they invariably hope for some kind of transcendence, some metaphysical assurance that will encompass that suffering and somehow redeem it ("How one hoped above, on and off," comments the speaker of "Text 2" from beyond the grave, "With what diversity"). Perhaps the most telling use of Beckett's implicit approach to religious imagery occurs in this pattern of guilt/judgment/salvation which underlies all of his major plays. In *Waiting for Godot*, for example, the first clearly explicit reference to salvation is found in Vladimir's mention of the two thieves crucified on either side of Christ, one of whom was saved and the other damned. But the tramps' interest in salvation is evident, on an implicit level, much earlier in the text, in their discussion of the state of Vladimir's kidneys. Through context or association, even the most neutral-sounding, seemingly unambiguous words may be charged with implicit religious significance:

Estragon: (*pointing*). You might button it all the same.
Vladimir: (*stooping*). True. (*He buttons his fly.*) Never neglect the little things of life.
Estragon: What do you expect, you always wait till the last moment.
Vladimir: (*musingly*). The last moment . . . (*He meditates.*) Hope deferred maketh the something sick, who said that?

"The last moment" is spoken by Estragon in all innocence, a perfectly straightforward and understandable reference to the fact that Vladimir habitually holds himself back from urinating. But the phrase contains an echo of Revelations' "The Last Judgment," and it is this association which causes Didi to "meditate," prompting the half-remembered Biblical proverb about the arrival of a hoped-for salvation. Similarly revealing is the statement from Didi that immediately follows: "Sometimes I feel it coming all the same. Then I go all queer. . . . How shall I say? Relieved and at the same time . . . appalled. (*With emphasis*.) AP-PALLED." Ostensibly, Vladimir is still talking about his mysterious kidney ailment; but, within the context of his having just brooded over "the last moment," the vagueness of "it" as a referent implies a significant ambiguity. The vehemence of his reaction (the particular strength of "appalled," both the word itself and the manner in which it is emphasized) suggests that what Didi is really talking about is his attitude to the prospect of divine judgment. (Note that the syllable breakup of "AP-PALLED," as specified by Beckett, stresses the "PALLED" by isolating it as a self-contained unit. "Pall" evokes the image of a hearse sheet, and so reinforces the implicit religious reference; death is precisely what Didi is afraid of.) Didi is "relieved" at the prospect of judgment, relieved that the waiting is finally over, but, at the same time, frightened that the judgment might go against him, frightened that it might signify his damnation.

It is also instructive to note the specific context in which Vladimir first mentions the thieves. Estragon's difficulty in removing his boot prompts Vladimir to observe: "There's man all over for you, blaming on his boots the faults of his feet. . . . This is getting alarming. . . . One of the thieves was saved. . . . Suppose we repented." Gogo is thus "guilty" in the matter of his feet [the original French stresses this element of guilt much more emphatically: "Voilà l'homme tout entier, s'en prenant à sa chaussure alors que c'est son pied *le coupable*" (italics added)]. But his guilt is not limited to this one specific, fairly trivial context; rather, it is a much wider, more inclusive, more significant guilt, a guilt Didi shares. It is Didi's brooding on this essentially theological guilt that causes the transition in his thoughts between feet and thieves, a transition similarly motivated in the exchange that follows almost immediately in the text:

> Vladimir: Where was I . . . How's your foot?
> Estragon: Swelling visibly.
> Vladimir: Ah yes, the two thieves.

"Foot" suggests "guilt," which in turn suggests "thieves." According to Vladimir's train of thought, the tramps are guilty, like the thieves, yet one of the thieves was saved. Perhaps if the tramps repented their "sins," they too might have a chance at divine salvation. ("Repented what? . . ." asks Estragon. "Our being born?")

Beckett is thus emphasizing the tramps' concern for salvation by implicitly *identifying* them with the thieves, in the above instance through the nuances of language. But Beckett is not restricted to the verbal plane. Thus, in the first act of *Waiting for Godot*, there is an extremely revealing tableau in which Gogo and Didi support between them the stricken Lucky: "*Vladimir and Estragon hoist Lucky to his feet, support him an instant, then let him go. He falls.*" An almost identical tableau occurs in Act II, except that now the character being supported by the tramps is the stricken Pozzo: "*They help Pozzo to his feet, let him go. He falls.*" The religious implications of the tramps' actions become evident only in the context of their prior discussion about the thieves. By flanking the suffering Lucky and Pozzo, the tramps are once more implicitly identified with the two thieves flanking the suffering Christ, an identification further strengthened by the verbal suggestiveness in both instances—Gogo's comment, "To hell with [Lucky]!" echoes the one thief's rejection of Christ, while Pozzo wonders whether the tramps on either side of him are "highwaymen". The tramps are thus shown to be spiritually precarious, like the thieves, concerned with the possibility of divine salvation.

The possibility of salvation is an issue of crucial importance in Beckett's plays; even more crucial, however, is the fact that it is a possibility continually frustrated. This destruction of the myth of salvation proceeds explicitly at the center of most Beckett's drama, but it also proceeds implicitly at the peripheries. When even the most trivial and mundane of dramatic passages, with apparently no religious reference at all, turns out to be commenting negatively on the chance for salvation, then that chance becomes more and more unlikely. Look, for example, at the passage describing Maddy Rooney's actions as she enters Mr. Slocum's car in the radio play *All That Fall*:

Mr. Slocum: (*Coolly*). May I then offer you a seat, Madam?
Mrs. Rooney: (*with exaggerated enthusiasm*). Oh that would be heavenly, Mr. Slocum, just simply heavenly. (*Dubiously*.) But would I ever get in, you look very high off the ground to-day, these new balloon tires, I presume. (*Sound of door opening and Mrs. Rooney trying to get in*.) . . . No . . . I'll never do it . . . you'll have to get down, Mr. Slocum, and help me from the rear. . . . Oh! . . Lower! . . Don't be afraid! . . We're past the age when . . . There! . . Now! . . Get your shoulder under it . . . Oh! . . (*Giggles*.) Oh glory! . . Up! Up! . . Ah! . . I'm in!

On the most immediate level, Maddy appears simply to be taking a seat in Mr. Slocum's automobile, obviously with some difficulty. It is well to remember, however, that the road on which Maddy is traveling is both geographically fixed and metaphorically symbolic—both the road that leads to the train station at Boghill and the road of life that leads to death and, possibly, salvation. (When Mr. Slocum stops to offer her a lift, he enquires, "Are you going in my direction?" to which Maddy replies, "I am, Mr. Slocum, we all are." Note, too, the progressively more sophisticated series of vehicles which appear on the road, from the simple cart through the more complex bicycle to the fully motorized car and van; clearly, this same road has existed throughout eternity.) On another level, then, Maddy's entering Mr. Slocum's car to travel along the road evokes the act of entering heaven. Maddy finds the entry arduous, the struggle is clearly an ascent ("Up! Up!"), she comments ambiguously "Oh glory!" and she wonders if, in fact, she will be able to get in.

But the hope of salvation is deflated by the deliberately mocking manner in which the ascent is parodied. For, on still another level, the ascent is ridiculed and vulgarized by being assimilated with the act of sexual intercourse. While Maddy is "heaving all over back and front," "dry" Mr. Slocum (the name is surely significant) tries his best, "I'm coming, Mrs. Rooney, I'm coming, give me time, I'm as stiff as yourself," and the consummation of their efforts is described by Maddy in deliciously ambiguous terms. The dream of paradise is thus exploded in outrageous burlesque. If salvation is doubtful, death and destruction are certain: "You'll get down, Mrs. Rooney, you'll get down. We may not get you up, but I warrant you we'll get you down".

If we wish to see Beckett's implicit approach to religious imagery in his drama at its most focused and undiluted, we have only to turn to *Embers*. This radio play has received relatively little critical attention over the years, perhaps because it is so strangely allusive and elusive. Most critics are baffled by it, and with some reason. But once we detect the pattern of implicit religious imagery which runs through the play —indeed, which *constitutes* the play—we are well on the way to piercing some of its mystery. Like so many of Beckett's plays, *Embers* dramatizes a quest for salvation, a quest which, as always, ultimately proves fruitless. Henry, the play's central character, is seeking salvation in the figure of his dead father, consistently identified in the play with Christ as a potential savior. Thus, if his father were to commune with Henry, his presence would constitute a resurrection: "My father, back from the dead, to be with me. . . . As if he hadn't died." Henry's father died by drowning at sea; in a poem called "Calvary By Night," included in the short story "A Wet Night," Beckett similarly depicts the death of Christ as a descent into water:

> the water
> the waste of water
>
> in the womb of water
> an pansy leaps
>
> rocket of bloom flare flower of night wilt for me
> on the breasts of the water it has closed it has made
> an act of floral presence on the water
> the tranquil act of its cycle on the waste
> from the spouting forth
> to the re-enwombing
> untroubled bow of petaline sweet-smellingness
> kingfisher abated
> drowned for me
> lamb of insustenance mine
>
> till the clamour of a blue bloom
> beat on the walls of the womb of
> the waste of
> the water

The sea in *Embers* becomes identified with the grave of Christ; as Henry himself comments:

> And I live on the brink of it! Why? Professional obligations? (*Brief laugh*.) Reasons of health? (*Brief laugh*.) Family ties? (*Brief laugh*.) A woman? (*Laugh in which [Ada] joins*.) Some old grave I cannot tear myself away from? (*Pause*.)

Henry's ironic laughs expose the absurdity of each of his proffered explanations—his living beside the sea has nothing to do with work, health, family, or women; since his wife Ada joins the last laugh, this confirms that Henry is not concerned with the sea because of her. But Henry's final suggestion is, significantly, *not* followed by a mocking, deflationary laugh, implying that here lies the true explanation. The presence of this sea-grave obsesses Henry, both repelling and attracting him at the same time. When Ada recalls that Henry's insistence on talking loudly in order to blot out the sound of the sea had puzzled and disturbed

their daughter, Henry replies, "I told you to tell her I was praying
. . . Roaring prayers at God and his saints". Praying is precisely what Henry is doing—pleading with his father, with Christ, to rise
up out of the water, to bring him salvation (six times Henry calls out
"Christ!").

Given this context, the significance of Henry's story about Bolton
and Holloway begins to emerge. Bolton's desperate plea to Holloway for
help mirrors the confrontation between Henry and his father. Bolton is
thus a surrogate for Henry—implicitly identified with Christ as sufferer.
Both his name (*Bolt*on) and the fact that he wears a red dressing gown (the
color is repeated three times in the text) link him with the Crucifixion
(before Christ was *nailed* to the cross, he was dressed in a *scarlet* robe).
And Holloway, the recipient of Bolton's supplication, is a surrogate for
Henry's father—implicitly identified with Christ as savior. Like Christ,
Holloway is a physician, a potential healer of men's souls. But the
identification is an ironic one. The Physician of the Gospels exclaimed,
"I am the way, the truth, and the life: no man cometh unto the Father, but
by me" (*John* 14:6); the physician of *Embers* is a *hollow*-way, a way
leading nowhere. And whereas Christ's death on the cross at "the ninth
hour" represents birth into a new life and the promise of salvation,
Holloway's actions, likewise at the ninth hour, result in the death of new
life, a universal *denial* of salvation: "If it's an injection you want,
Bolton, let down your trousers and I'll give you one, I have a
panhysterectomy at *nine*" (italics added).

The confrontation between Bolton and Holloway is thus a paradigm
of human suffering and divine rejection:

> That's it, that was always it, night, and the embers cold, and the glim
> shaking in your old fist, saying, Please! Please! (*Pause*.) Begging. (*Pause*.)
> Of the poor. (*Pause*.) Ada! (*Pause*.) Father! (*Pause*.) Christ!
> (*Pause*.) . . . Holloway covers his face, not a sound, . . . no good.
> (*Pause*.) No good. (*Pause*.) Christ!

Like Bolton, Henry is "begging" of the "poor—of Ada, of his father,
ultimately of Christ. (Ada is implicitly linked with Henry's father
throughout the play. Both are associated with the sound of hooves; both
are addressed by Henry with the same phrase, "Be with me"; and Ada's
name is a near anagram for "Dad," just as its diminutive borne by her
daughter is an exact rhyme: Daddy! Addie!) But being "poor," they are
spiritually empty; the result is "no good." Henry's final speech em-
phasizes the utter futility of his quest:

> This evening . . . (*Pause.*) Nothing this evening. (*Pause.*)
> Tomorrow . . . tomorrow . . . plumber at nine, then nothing. (*Pause.*
> *Puzzled.*) Plumber at nine? (*Pause.*) Ah yes, the waste. (*Pause.*) Words.
> Saturday . . . nothing. Sunday . . . Sunday . . . nothing all day.
> (*Pause.*) Nothing, all day nothing. (*Pause.*) All day all night nothing.
> (*Pause.*) Not a sound.
> (*Sea.*)

Henry's comment "words" might just as well have been "play-on-words," for the entire passage works on two levels. Keeping in mind the image of Christ's death as a descent into water, the "plumber" is thus seen to refer to Jesus, who was crucified on Friday at the ninth hour. Christ therefore "plumbs" the waste ("the waste / the waste of water"). But "waste" also refers to the significance of his death. For on Saturday, the day of waiting, there is nothing; but there is likewise nothing on Sunday, the day of resurrection, the day on which Christ should rise from the dead and regain paradise for man. Christ's silence ("All day all night nothing. . . . Not a sound") is the silence of Henry's father, the silence of the sea; as Ada had warned Henry, using the identical words: "Underneath [the sea] all is as quiet as the *grave*. Not a sound. *All day, all night, not a sound*" (italics added). That *Embers* ends with the sound of the sea is therefore highly ironic, for the sound is an empty one, containing no message of spiritual consolation. Henry's father will never rise up; the voice that would promise salvation is silent.

The plays of Samuel Beckett abound in religious (particularly Christian) imagery and thought. As Beckett himself has remarked: "Christianity is a mythology with which I am perfectly familiar, so I naturally use it." But to conclude, therefore, that Beckett is a Christian dramatist—if one means by that statement that he espouses an essentially Christian point of view, and not simply that he deals with certain obviously Christian motifs—is surely to misjudge on the most fundamental level the significance of the plays' religious reference. Far from offering hope of religious consolation, Beckett's drama is a *kyrie eleison* of suffering and despair, in which anguished cries of spiritual emptiness alternate with a bitterly outraged and frequently outrageous indictment of the extent of divine malevolence. Instead of providing support for a Christian interpretation, the presence of Biblical imagery in the play serves rather to undermine such an interpretation through ironic counterpoint. For the thrust of Beckett's religious reference suggests that man is the victim of a heartless metaphysical ruse, trapped in the midst of an alien and hostile world, his life a protracted and painful crucifixion without hope of transcendence. Each element of Beckett's dramatic art isolates, and thus reinforces, these same central thematic issues—the universality of suffering and the impossibility of salvation.

Before one can interpret the meaning of religious imagery in Beckett's plays, however, one must first be able to detect its presence. "In the beginning was the pun," quips the eponymous hero of Beckett's novel *Murphy*, a line that could easily serve as a critical introduction to both the content and the form of Beckett's drama. For the line is both a parody of a specific Biblical text, the opening words of the Gospel According to Saint John, and an indication of how Beckett frequently makes us aware of such religious reference in his work: the "word" is replaced by the "pun," the play-on-words, the double or even triple significance. Such nuances are not confined only to the verbal level in Beckett's drama; implicit religious reference is also conveyed through the suggestiveness of visual elements like set, costuming, and gesture.

The approach of Beckett's drama to issues of religious concern is thus oblique. This is not to imply, of course, that the plays do not contain explicit religious imagery, for clearly they do. Rather, it is that they dramatize religious issues more frequently than one might at first assume, more frequently than a superficial glance at the text might indicate. On the surface, the drama often seems to be dealing with only the most trivial, the most commonplace of topics, topics with no apparent religious significance at all. There is nothing inherently religious about a dustbin, for example, or the word "plumber," or the action of getting into a car. As we have seen, however, the surface is deceptive, for through verbal and visual suggestiveness, such images become rich in implicit religious relevance. In a letter to Alan Schneider, Beckett once observed about *Endgame*: "Rather difficult and elliptic, mostly depending on the power of the text to claw." Beckett's plays "claw" because they set off haunting reverberations, because each of the elements of his drama invariably suggests so much more than it at first seems to. And it is precisely this wedding of the implicit with the explicit that provides Beckett's drama with its extraordinary religious density, the wellspring of both its beauty and its power.

Place of Narration/Narration of Place

Work	Place where story is told	Narrator
More Pricks	extratextual	nonparticipating witness
Murphy	extratextual	nonparticipating
Watt	extratextual but witnessed in text	witness manifested during narration
Mercier et Camier	extratextual	witness manifested at the start
Stories	extratextual	first person
Molloy	intratextual and stationary	first person (personal)
Malone Dies	intratextual and stationary	first person (personal)
The Unnamable	intratextual and mobile	first person (impersonal)
Texts for Nothing	intratextual and mobile	first person (impersonal)
From an Abandoned Work	extratextual	first person
How It Is	extratextual extratextual notebook denied intratextual intratextual by the end	unvoiced, depersonalized first person
Enough	extratextual but situated by the text in a "down there'	first person
Imagination Dead	extratextual	nonparticipating
The Lost Ones	extratextual	nonparticipating
Ping	extratextual	nonparticipating
Lessness	extratextual	nonparticipating

Cause of displacement	Who is displaced?	Kinds of places
necessary, without further explanation ("Ding-Dong")	third person protagonist	Ireland, country and city
flight from others and search for particular kind of place	third person protagonist	Cork, Dublin, London, refuge
unmotivated	third person protagonist	two places of refuge (one nameless) between journeys
unmotivated	third person protagonist	trips through a city (Dublin stylized) and nameless countryside
after expulsion or unmotivated flight, search for particular kind of place	first person protagonists	from nameless foreign city to personal room and container
to find his mother's room	first person protagonist	city country forest (room)
unmotivated	avatars of the narrator	city country refuge (room)
unmotivated	avatars of the narrator	abstract circular space (jar), a few Parisian names
unmotivated	(nameless) avatars of the narrator	exploded abstract space, a few Irish and Parisian names
to leave his mother's house	first person protagonist	countryside (Irish) of childhood
unmotivated and generalized	first person protagonist	mud down there (light above)
unmotivated	couple protagonist	earth, flowers, sky
no further displacement		white rotunda
search for an improbable exit	third person population	cylinder, yellow light
either no displacement or sudden, almost invisible displacement	third person protagonist	cube, white light
unmotivated, in the future	third person protagonist	ruins, wholly gray space

Ludovic Janvier

Place of Narration/Narration of Place

I DESIGNATION OF THE LANDSCAPE

Let us examine two related kinds of place in fiction. We will call one kind the "place of narration," where the actual telling takes place. The other kind, the "narration of place," is the story setting, where landscapes, characters, gestures, and activities are situated. This distinction is obvious in *Molloy*. The place of narration is the room in which the narrator writes, as described in the first words of the text. It is the place in which, recalling his journey to reach the room, he tells about himself without ever leaving the room. The narration of place is the description of this journey, the discourse of this recollection; we see Molloy wandering from public places to shelters, from shelters to forests, from forests to the room, that enclosed place from which his account will depart, without departing. It is interesting to trace the link between the situation of narration and the journey of the character, or rather, between the situation of the narrating character (Molloy writing here and now) and the wandering of the narrated character (Molloy written in the past). Activity and retroactivity, mobility and immobility are reciprocal functions; thus the seeming artifice of the discourse is its greatest truth—to tell about the departure toward the self, i.e., toward a place that is always there, since that alone permits the discourse about this journey. Beckett himself confirms it: "I conceived Molloy and the rest the day I became conscious of my stupidity. Then I began to write the things that I feel." That discovery and that decision are faithfully imitated by Molloy. At the moment that the writer anchors the narrator, that narrator is charged with staging the detour of the very process of writing.

The link between narration of place and place of narration is illuminated, on the one hand, by examination of the textual basis of narration (Molloy tells his own story, but who tells Murphy's story?) and, on the other hand, by examination of various background elements—cause of displacement, who is displaced, kinds of places traversed (in *Malone Dies*, Malone speaks, but it is not he who moves), and duration of the itinerary.

For each Beckett work or group of related works, we can designate the situation of the narration—an invented place and a character in that place. Examination of these perspectives should afford a total view of the spatial structure of the text. This can be arranged in a table in which vertical and/or horizontal reading allows us to follow diachronically and/or synchronically both the story and the system of "Beckettian places." We will comment on this table, and this table will comment on our account.

The whole might be considered a systematization of commentaries about dwelling, voyaging, carrying on a discourse—commentaries that other critics have made or implied. But the whole may furnish the basis for a theory of what we will tentatively call the the relationship between fixing in words and fixing in location.

II DESCRIPTION OF THE WORKS

A. *More Pricks Than Kicks, Murphy, Watt,* and *Mercier* and *Camier* share certain characteristics that separate them from the rest of the Beckett canon. These texts of 1934 to 1945 may be called "distant narratives." Since the place of narration is not designated, let us call it "extratextual," as is true of most objective third person accounts. But this objectivity (activated by an agent or actant of narration) sometimes looks like an ill-fitting mask over a nameless subjectivity. Extratextual though he may be, the narrator of *More Pricks* intrudes into the story, "My sometime friend Belacqua," he says at the beginning of "Ding-Dong." Or he plays at guiding the reader: "Reader, a coffee is laced with brandy," in "Love and Lethe." Or, in "Walking Out," he chats like an experienced novelist: "Yet we feel we must say before we let her be, her poor body that must wither that her nether limbs, from where they began even until where they ended, would have done credit to a Signorelli page."

The extratextuality is sustained, but the apparent narrative objectivity is slightly disturbed by these ironies, as though there were some difficulty in maintaining distance, in spite of the choice of the third person. What is probably being revealed is the profound complicity between narrator and narrated (the actant of narration confronted by Belacqua), so that the former leans toward the latter.

Written a few years later, *Watt* and *Mercier and Camier* go further; though the originating point of narration is still invisible, the account is attributed to a witness indicated by the narrative and participating in the action. In *Watt* there are notes that hint at the method of narration; the text supplies its own archeology. Most important is the author explicitly named Sam (Beckett's own name), who appears in the third part of the novel, not only to hear Watt's story, which he will report (and which will constitute the novel), but also to accompany the "hero." (And yet, the objective account is improbable, if not impossible, since it deals with events which Watt has just noted and therefore could not report to the narrator, and which we therefore learn from an anonymous author, temporarily ill at ease in his distance.) We are left with a moving *pair* of protagonists, impelled toward one another by solitude and tenderness. This first couple in Beckett's narration is a major event in the relationship between narrator and narrated. The source of the story has drawn close enough to its object, the character, to touch it. There is still a space-time separation in the actual delivery of the story, but the couple is a major technical advance in these distant narratives, an advance which *Mercier and Camier* treats in its own way. One might think this first French novel a step backward from *Watt*, as though it were necessary in this new itinerary to take off from a higher point without safety rails. But this fragile, hesitant text opens with abrupt words that situate the narrator in the immediate proximity of a faithful companion, and this time from beginning to end of the story: "The voyage of Mercier and Camier is one I can tell if I wish, for I was with them all the time." The narrative leans toward its anchor.

And what of narration of place? The four texts share the organic and unmotivated necessity of wandering. In "Ding-Dong," we find the best description of the cause of displacement—a sybilline hint of a strange condition and sense of well-being:

> My sometime friend Belacqua enlivened the last phase of his solipsism, before he toed the line and began to relish the world, with the belief that the best thing he had to do was to move constantly from place to place. He did not know how this conclusion had been gained, but that it was not thanks to his preferring one place to another he felt sure. He was pleased to

think that he could give what he called the Furies the slip by merely setting himself in motion. But as for sites, one was as good as another, because they all disappeared as soon as he came to rest in them. The mere act of rising and going, irrespective of whence and whither, did him good. That was so.

These four texts also share a third person account of a character or couple who journeys, tries to rest, and is finally left to its fate.

However, they differ by pairs in two essential points: (1) *More Pricks* and *Murphy* take place in recognizable parts of Ireland—Dublin or the Wicklow countryside. The abundance of proper names resembles a collage in that the books straddle two worlds, external and internal. In contrast, *Mercier and Camier* and especially *Watt* consist of discourses that are gradually stripped of geographic and social reference. A few residual traces of Dublin and countryside remain, but reality is dissolving as though an anchor were raised, permitting the work to set out slowly toward its own myth. Belacqua and Murphy traverse our world, the former to die "misunderstood," the latter to die in an asylum. Mercier, Camier, and Watt hesitate, go in circles, rest for a time, set out again. They are free of ties, gliding this way or that. (2) At the end of their linear and "realistic" itineraries, Belacqua and Murphy die. Watt, Mercier, and Camier survive at the temporary end of their less active wandering. On the one hand, death is linked to a voyage through our world; on the other, survival is linked to an anchorage in a mythical place. To spare the characters a facile fate incommensurate with their courage and modesty, the narrative contrives these zones that are still somewhat troubled but already sheltered—zones in which the characters gradually abate their activity. The narrator discreetly imitates the solicitude of the narrative: "I was with them all the time."

B. The approach has been made, if indeed narrator and narrated have not actually met. The four stories written at about the same time as *Mercier and Camier* (1945 to 1946) are an important step forward. A transitional phase, they prepare the change that is clearly predicted in *The Calmative*, the last of the four to be written. The stories differ both from the first works and from those that follow.

Though the place of narration is neither designated nor implied by the text, the time of narration may be viewed as a kind of localization. In *The Expelled*, the moment of telling tends to join the act of telling —or rather, the "having told"—to the concrete text. "I don't know why I told this story. I could just as well have told another," says the narrator at the end. As for the narrator of *The Calmative*, from the first words of his discursive journey he describes his post mortem situation. One might say: time of after-time, place of non-place; therefore, extratextual time and place. But indicated in the text as well as indicating the text, this time of after-telling and this unnamed place are the refuge and shelter toward which the writing progresses. We are only at the threshold of the present of invention, but the narrative indications have brought us to that point.

This is the crucial authorial decision that makes possible a confessional narrative; from now on the actant of narration is also its object. Character and narrator are blended so that the function of the one is to recount himself in the other. It is impossible to distinguish the two remarkable traits that define the place of narration: (1) the narrative account is like a future tense describing a space that is immanent but still has to be defined; (2) by the ruse of the past tense, the subject predicts a self-story in which the character will stage his own life.

If we examine the patterns of narration of place, we discover a conflict between wandering and shelter, inaugurated by the preceding texts. Murphy died in his shelter, and Watt left it. Now the character-narrator, speaking in the first person, states and restates his distaste for the vertical and his taste for a shelter far from others; he sinks into it, he gives up, he withdraws. *The Expelled*, or the loss of enclosed space. *The End*, or its reconquest: "I longed to be under cover again, in an empty place, close and warm, with artificial light." All his displacements are tense with desire and regret; all associations—human, animal, natural—are animated by the same fear of others and by the same obsession with withdrawal. Places dwindle and grow empty; passions desert them; they are shaped to the dimension and immediate needs of the character. The city? It no longer has a name, and it is puzzling even to someone born there (*The Expelled*). It is a place upon which an activity and a history are projected, but the history cannot be deciphered (*The End*). The country? Motionless, stylized, always the same. But there are rooms, stables, caves, and finally a canoe—variants of the archetypical form, a box in which to protect oneself, to undo oneself, a second and solid skin as buffer against a world that is too big. The survival of these questers (in *The Expelled*, *The Calmative*, and *First Love*) is not without hope in the temptation to end; (in *The End*) hope of a death is drawn to desired dimensions.

Thus the junction of the two selves takes place in a womblike place. Or rather, when that junction is about to occur, after all the torments and delays, it is dissolved by death—the canoe of *The End* (which is why Beckett reordered the sequence, irrespective of the chronology of its creation, placing *The End* at the end). The chosen place could not be inhabited; it is not yet the right size for the seeker. But is there a habitable space for him?

C. A singular and remarkable archipelago is formed by *Molloy*, *Malone Dies*, *The Unnamable* (the trilogy), to which should be added the thirteen *Texts for Nothing*. In this third movement, we are at the threshold of the undertaking whose progress we have followed from work to work. The place of narration is designated by the text, secreted by it. The place of departure for *Molloy* and *Malone Dies* is the motionless space of a room, a kind of balcony in eternity from which narrator and reader watch a tour through space-time. It seems possible to dwell there *in order to* write. The stable place is no longer one of death or cessation as in *Watt* or the *Stories*; it is not abandoned, but it provides a platform from which to unwind; one speaks from the fixed point it presents—beginning and end of the double journey, written and fictitious. But misgivings gnaw at the writing, which becomes the motivating force of *The Unnamable* and the *Texts for Nothing*.

The text declares itself the only reality and the only conceivable space. In *The Unnamable*, place descriptions contradict each other or are telescoped within the larger prespective of the narrative, so that the action of writing becomes the only place for the existent searching with words. In *Texts for Nothing*, we have the diaspora, a declaration of aporia, constant self-contradiction. The only sustained and persistent place is the concatenation of the discourse, continued as soon as dropped by a homeless narrator, or rather by a narrator making his domicile in the discontinuous trail that he inscribes before our eyes and his own. In this progression from *Molloy* to the *Texts for Nothing*, from a "human" place in the text to the text as non-place, we must recognize the end of that itinerary leading from *Murphy* to *Watt*, from *Watt* to *The Calmative*, from *The Calmative* to *Molloy*; from a text about reality to the sole reality of the text; from writing as the only possible shelter to writing, the non-shelter.

In the context of a namable and circumscribed setting, the subject is, quite logically, personal. He speaks in his own name (even if he sometimes forgets it, as does Molloy whose omissions and corrections indicate his precarious state) in the place where he has finally arrived, as if buttressed by his discourse. That is the posture of Molloy and Malone. But all guides disintegrate when the signposts prove factitious as the story unwinds, and when place is reduced to the continuously open totality of the writing, with the narrator shuttling tirelessly to and from himself. Identity has to be created, proved by words. Noun and pronoun can no longer mask or reveal the vacancy. The subject is now impersonal, clothed in cast-off rags; in *The Unnamable* he decks himself out elegantly in the uncertain identities of Mahood and Worm, all the better "to exist." Or he is anonymous and maskless, like the name-

less, personless, thingless being who causes the bottomless sky to gravi-
tate about his absence in *Texts for Nothing*. The place of narration is the
developing non-place of narration, lacking a center.

But the narration of place? It is the narration of the place of others,
except for Molloy and Moran whose journeys are motivated. They live
their itineraries in the past tense, so that the reader can recapitulate their
wandering but charted existence, which leads them to that point of flight
and meeting where the writing is anchored in the strangeness of self.
Molloy and Moran steal away from themselves, but they do so consciously, and not without containing in the circle of their words the
whole circle of their personal quest—hope of reaching the self, of
resting in the self, of departing again from the self toward the end of
every quest. Burdened with this heritage, the subsequent "heroes"
wander and rest by proxy. In their discourses, others have the mission of
traversing places—city and mythic country that they themselves can
only envisage. They are immobile, derisively imitating the central but
impotent position in which they are placed by the hope, then the failure
of every meeting. What space is invented for these erect beings by the
existent who is prone, or moldy, or nowhere! Circles, then spirals, or
open circles. "Then I resumed my spirals," announced Molloy, although he was certain—in retrospect, or rather in the prologue of his
narrative—of the providential stability of the room in which he wrote.
And the Unnamable: "I must have got embroiled in a kind of inverted
spiral, I mean one of the coils of which, instead of widening more and
more, grew narrower and narrower and finally, given the kind of space
in which I was supposed to evolve, would come to an end for lack of
room." The desired center may be the unattainable present of the writing, which is hidden by the very act of writing. The written text can tell
only what has already been written; it is condemned to be read. The
distance covered can reflect only what has already been covered. Alone
outside of the text but moving it forward, the subject is absent. Of this
absence in space, the Unnamable speaks continuously, but with borrowed names and places. The *Texts for Nothing* frankly describe a
mythic and mobile space whose freedom is reflected in a text whose
only hope is to endure long enough to speak, thus delaying the movement toward death, that final point in a story about a "life" totally
stolen by an elsewhere.

In the discursive space common to all these moving beings, where
position and identity are about to cease or prove a lie, how can we speak
of "taking place?" Turned back upon itself so as to be described in an
event without end, the narrative can only pass through places. In the
rage of pursuing itself while declaring the risks of such pursuit, the

narrative can only traverse sites which, scarcely situated, are at once
denied. For someone gnawed by the desire for self, there is no possible
dwelling. (*Malone Dies*. "De born, that's the brainwave now." *The
Unnamable*: "You must say words, as long as there are any, until they
find me.") Subjectless subject, placeless place, no rest. There is a story
in four stages of a dwelling diffused into endless loss. If for Molloy, the
ancestor of these narrators, the narration of place departs from and
returns to the place of narration, the room, the alpha and omega of the
circular text, his anonymous descendant in the *Texts for Nothing* is
condemned to step after exhausted step in a relentless flight forward.
The one is a boomerang, the other a wasted shot. The written text is
forever a detour. Writing, or thirteen blows for *nothing*.

   D. It is unnecessary to comment on Beckett's fictional silence
after *Texts for Nothing*, which the author himself admitted as having
failed to extricate him from the closed narrative circle of *The
Unnamable*. Because the narrative tried to capture the writing writer in
the very movement of his writing, with the aim of stretching narrator
and narrative toward a vanishing point, the undertaking could only
begin endlessly again and again. "You must go on . . . I'll go on" are
the gears of a discourse that can barely continue or that breaks down
completely.

   The recourse to theater can be explained by faith—*credo quia
absurdum*—in a certain space, in a minimal identity, in a durability that
will not disintegrate word by word. Faith, in short, in all these methods
of arresting hemorrhage. One must be silent or be able to continue
speaking. In order to continue speaking, here are the safety rails and
limits. Such is Beckett's theater, from an immovable space to a prudent
discourse, even when it is destructive; it is an ante-purgatory in which
the writer, worn out, rests his language and stabilizes his creatures. No
longer focused on the self, but seeing and hearing oneself. No longer
seeking oneself through a faithless discourse, but waiting, enduring,
dwelling in time, with the help of a faithful discourse and of other
beings in flesh and words. The *Texts for Nothing* was the closest approach to a secret but untenable home. The theater strays from it,
retreating toward a less exposed zone, where the suffering will no
longer spring exclusively from the threat of asphyxiation in speaking of
the self in the words of others—"strange punishment, strange sin."
Slow ebb.

   In the temporal explosion of texts as different as *How It Is* (1960)
and *From an Abandoned Work* (1957), *Enough* and *Ping* (1966),
Imagination Dead Imagine (1965), *The Lost Ones* (written 1966; published 1970), and *Lessness* (1969), a withdrawal is evident in the very

dispersal of texts, as in their reduced size and the fierce concentration of the writing. No longer logorrheal panic but brief gasps; elocution by spasms and ellipses. The era of fluency is over. Prudently, then, we use our two exploratory perspectives that are almost too convenient.

From an Abandoned Work, *How It Is*, and *Enough* (a throwback, though written after *Imagination Dead*) should be grouped together because of their centrifugal movement. In them, setting appears as a ruse of the discourse. *From an Abandoned Work* is neither set in its text, like *The Unnamable*, nor in a recognizable place, like *Molloy*. But certain hints—above all the repeated beginnings of a narrator at once pressed to finish and lingering over details—reveal that this self-confessedly capricious account is an exact parallel to the *Stories* in its subject who is anonymous but preoccupied with his genealogy, who is the subject of his story but at some distance from the text we read. This subject, like that of the *Stories*, recapitulates (with tension and ellipses) three days of wandering and of childish anxieties, which have made him what he is. The subject is again in an Irish countryside, atypical but recognizable; again he engages in human occupations; but he moves off into this unfinished confession with its unbearable focal point. The fact that it is unfinished implies that these rediscoveries with their referential reality are at once urgent and temporary; this renewal of resources serves the better to redisappear into myth and rage. But a major truce is marked by this abrupt release of a childhood country, sketched in a few pages by a narrator flirting with his pain and his exile. More than a resting place, it marks the beginning of peace with that consuming obsession of seizing oneself in the very process of the discourse.

How It Is is the return to myth, with the same narrative ambiguity. The narration of place is a return to myth about a larval creature, narrated and narrating, plunged with his fellow creatures in ubiquitous mud. But in that mud the creature moves in his own name, following an interminable procession from west to east, finally opening out into an unexpected universal dimension, since all humanity seems to be crawling eastward toward a problematical birth. The subject is trying "to exist." On the one hand, for him there is no longer an anchorage, a room, a fixed point, a desired center, an origin. On the other hand, there is no longer self-torment, but progress, with the help of a fellow creature, and there is the necessity to use up time and space. With the same movement, the subject is first alone (Part I), then in a couple (Part 2), and finally drowned in a multitude (Part 3); the return to myth yields a new myth that terminates that absolute and monadic singularity in which the trilogy imprisoned the windowless existent. To begin wandering again is to free oneself from the reflexive reduction to which even the wanderer Molloy was a prey. There is an ambulatory unwinding in *How It Is*, where the human larva, yard by yard, joins his fellow creatures in patiently re-creating the human terrain. The mud through which one advances so little and so badly is a sticky element, an all-inclusive place of relentless punishment; but it is also a wide-open space permitting slow progress that is free of preoccupations with goal, origin, or return. Glued to the mud because he is trapped in time, the crawling creature suffers, but he relaxes from hoping, for he is without illusions; he pants, but he is no longer driven to seek the grace of the last word. Though the mire probably reflects the abode of the Greedy and the Prodigal of Dante's *Inferno*, the crawling is an extension of that strange metaphor inherited from Geulincx, which appears in *Molloy*: "I who had loved the image of old Geulincx, dead young, who left me free, on the black boat of Ulysses, to crawl towards the East along the deck. . . . And from the poop, poring upon the wave, a sadly rejoicing slave, I follow with my eyes the proud and futile wake. Which, as it bears me from no fatherland away, bears me onward to no shipwreck." A route within prison, but freedom through that route; thus, from the pride that makes the creature sign in the mud, there arises the design necessary to his life.

We find a similar pattern in *Enough*: this time it is a couple who wanders (with the narrating "I," its beginning and end) through a distance commensurate with the size of the globe—several times around an equator. This is a step forward toward flight, but the narrative knowingly substitutes that flight for an illusory advance toward the self. At the same time, this work is a farewell to voyages whose amazing extent finally finalizes the consuming but exhausted mobility of the exile; and it hints at the immobility of the infinitely small in which the narrative will soon be enclosed. We are learning to recognize this flux and reflux in Beckett.

But the place of narration is ambiguous. The narrated protagonist of *How It Is* does not seem to be the narrator, who states that all his actions are noted by a scribe. It is the obverse of *The Unnamable*: events involving the subject are narrated by another, that extratextual bookkeeper mentioned in the text. Moreover, the subject often indicates that he is quoting, as a virtual refrain. He is merely transmitting, imbued with the message and possessed by the offstage writer. But the textual tissue passes through him—a last need for anchoring, which can be viewed as a special dwelling of the narrative discourse: if the narrative lacks a place here, where there is pain and panting, there can be no respite for writing, but there is respite for listening and murmuring. The speaker is a loudspeaker; the subject is literally "inspired" to speak. This dichotomy or scissiparity characterizes a last effort to cast light on the separation in a first person narrative: the one who "lives" down there in the writing "is lived" up here in the very act of writing. And then the exigencies of truth cause the narrator to say that it is all fiction and "all balls"—these inventions of notebook and scribe, God and the others. Thus, there is reestablishment in realistic isolation of the writer at work, where delegation of power and activity has again enabled the narrative to cross the desert. A strategic lie becomes the truth of fatigue. This shuttling denies both wandering and fixity. The narrative subject will no longer attack his own shadow, but he has to lie a little if he wants to construct a dwelling. Once built, it is abandoned. Both inside and outside the action, the narrator is scissiparous of himself, but he is the only one there. If he wants to sign his own story, he has to spare himself, and yet he wears himself out in so doing. At the other end of his pen is that donné that he takes up again, that was and remains made of words. Adieu. An adieu confirmed by *Enough*; the anonymous pen that is activated in the first words of the text is the one that says "Enough" in the last words. Enough seeing oneself, enough telling oneself. Rest; the subject is at an end. Exhaustion not of telling but of telling oneself. Not of writing but of writing into an interminable future. Violence committed, the oeuvre now becomes a series of brief flashes, without loss or flux, but brilliant with concentrated light.

The second group consists of *Imagination Dead Imagine*, *Ping*, *The Lost Ones*, and *Lessness*—enclosed works since the narration of place grants to the invented moribund a parsimonious space in which movement is reduced or infinitesimal, in which immobility looks like death, in which light is overpowering as though to prevent any hope of shade, i.e., any hope of hope. As for the place of narration: all discursive action withdraws outside the text, for resumption of third-person distance indicates the end of a suffering rendered plausible by the strategies of *How It Is* and *Enough*. The narrator has disappeared; there is only the narration, purified of the tricks of *More Pricks*.

In its new, anonymous course, a route of flashes, what does the text invent? Fortified shelters—incomprehensible unless one has followed the painful journey through times, landscapes, and temporary dwellings—of someone who thought he could build a home of words around his lack of being. But one cannot build on a lack; one withdraws. The narration is put to another purpose; from a distance it watches a closed-off world where hope is minimally and literally illusion, a world in which creatures bled white have surrendered all their (slender) qualities for the beautiful and perfect clarity of a language bordering on the rare grace of the abstract. Cylinder, sphere, cube in which white rules; these colorless and almost historyless places recall the flat luminosity of Mondrian, to make a common comparison. They are purged of much flesh, of many words, of almost all drama. Those who live there seem to be in an afterlife, in a purgatorial light. Motion is as imperceptible as blinking. Spaces are flawlessly smooth. In comparison, the mud of *How It Is* is full of future, since one moves forward, and the jar of *The Unnamable* is a platform of promises. But here all hope is imprisoned; places are without a future. People pass by one another (*The Lost Ones*), they sleep (*Imagination Dead*), they scarcely breathe (*Ping*) as though in a hell jar or a dream. Of if the place remains open—a departure point for an elusive existence—it is on sand or cinders of a near and fragile future. This landscape is as impalpable as the difficult breathing of the nameless, wordless creature who, we might guess, is in no hurry to set foot on it, after so many wounds and prisons. Here is the beginning of *Lessness*: "Ruins true refuge long last towards which so many false time out of mind. All sides endlessness earth sky as one no sound no stir. Grey face two pale blue little body heart beating only upright. Blacked out fallen open four walls over backwards true refuge issueless." This is the almost fireless, placeless pattern carried by the narrative, as though freed from narrative. Fireless for there is no one, placeless for the refuge is in ruins; or more exactly, the person consists of dry elements without syntactical cement. If these pieces first enclose then cautiously free these vague specters (with the alternation previously noted), it is through the exigencies of a style that is without pathos and that is fascinating in its poverty. Without rejecting a narrative, or at least a descriptive content, the post-dramatic texts tend increasingly toward this voluntary asceticism and this controlled violence, which finally eliminates pain and hope—everything that impeded the flow of this dry, cruel, brisk, hard discourse. Concentrated in these narratives, the texts are as impenetrable as pebbles. It is for the sake of the language that Beckettian narration has invented strange beings, approached them, put them in a room, a box, a cage in which to speak for them; then the narrative has left them, seen them from a distance where they have retreated to almost nothing in the almost nothing of a retreat apart from all story.

III THE TEMPLE

Writing, who can say he is building? Or having written, that he has mastery over place? In a dwelling, who shelters whom? Words are not dwellings; speaking, I am always outside myself. And yet the theater of words is a dwelling; they create space, an enclosure, an absolute exterior that is within, a tomb. In the inmost part of this enclosure is myself, that other. Myself, that other, in "the square space marked by prophecy in heaven and on earth, in the interior of which omens are seen and interpreted." This is the first description of a temple (quoted from a Latin dictionary), and it will serve for the textual temple cut out of and again enclosed in the vast ever-open space of world-language in which the story subject suffers, once again.

How else can this persistent fetish of the Refuge be viewed, unless the operator of the writing is himself seen in this commonplace word that opens him to the world and leaves him exposed? Because this word is the story, and because this story inter-dicts me—my body, the water, the sky, you, me—I do not take place; I follow my course. I own nothing; I lack. In the wide open space, nothing suits me; I am afraid. For the subject-who-moves-speaking, everything opens endlessly into a quasiworld that has already been spoken. Whether I accept the interdiction or talk to myself, confined to the words that formulate my law and that of the world, let us contemplate this idol that is finally bereft of me and that gives me back to myself—my text, this temple. Or to phrase it differently: from my body language frightened by the law, I drop words. This is perfect human production with the appearance of reproduction—to compose a space in which a being of language will issue from me. For that moment, farewell to fear in the endless process. It is my word, against the world. It is contemplated, whereas the world is outside the sanctuary. I will make the law, a law written about the world, which my word has silenced. I have stolen the declarer of law. In the story-world I may be displaced, destroyed, confined to utopias, but in the temple of the text (even when it traces routes and journeys), I give to my images the paradoxical play of a process that is a dwelling, of a utopia that is a positioning.

Living: seized backward in the story whose landscape takes on order in spite of me. Me, spoken thing.

Textual: conclusive origin of a narrator who uses language to situate a toppled image of a body in the course of destruction. That I may draw it into a dead transparency of words. Me, speaking master.

Yes, the words-without-me carry me into the world, all the better to turn against the world the certainty of order—*their* order which is never fortuitous. That certainty must be renewed? I renew it. I leave again for my resting place, I make words again, I cut them out, I inscribe. Death will find me at my feverish busywork of making a little order in the middle of my own little square. Good.

Elin Diamond

"what? . . . who? . . . no! . . . she!" –
The Fictionalizers in Beckett's Plays

The unhealthy and often immobile protagonists in Beckett's plays are vitally creative individuals; they have to be. Trapped in barren comfortless worlds, hounded by mortality, their existence in present time is almost unendurable. But in present time they must exist and find the means to survive.

For three of Beckett's protagonists, Hamm in *Endgame*, Winnie in *Happy Days*, and the Mouth in *Not I*, one means of survival is fictionalizing. Hamm, Winnie, and the Mouth create fictions in an attempt to remove themselves from the reality of the present. Their impulse to fictionalize is the impulse to recreate the self or "I," which, because time-bound, exists in a state of mental torment and physical degeneration. For all three storytellers, the fictions are an attempt to supply what is lacking in their actual existence: for Hamm, the ability to end; for Winnie, the ability to act and effect action; for the Mouth, the ability to objectify experience. The fictions are heroic attempts, but they are, finally, failures. Storytelling relieves but does not cure the pains of existence.

Present reality is, for Hamm, a purgatory of hesitation. Though master of the shelter (presumably the last place of human habitation) and chief player of the endgame, Hamm's first soliloquy shows him stymied.

> Enough, it's time it ended, in the shelter, too. (*Pause.*)
> And yet I hesitate, I hesitate to . . . to end. Yes, there it is, it's time it ended
> and yet I hesitate to—(*he yawns*)
> —to end.

111

Yawning is just one of the ways in which Hamm stalls. He orders Clov to inspect the landscape, to push him around the room, and when tired of these occupations, he insists on the "dialogue": "Ah, the old questions, the old answers, there's nothing like them." Hamm perceives the necessity for ending; human life with its suffering must not continue, yet he is lured into hesitation by the thought that "perhaps it won't all have been for nothing."

Life in the shelter, however, is approaching nothing. The servant Clov apparently has shrunk; he has to use a ladder in order to see out of the windows. Hamm's parents, Nagg and Nell, are legless, residing in ashbins. Hamm himself is blind, confined to a wheelchair, and, as he tells Clov, bleeding "less." Hamm dreams of health and mobility, only to return to his own state of degeneration.

> If I could sleep I might make love. I'd go into the woods. My eyes would see . . . the sky, the earth.
> I'd run, run, they wouldn't catch me.
> (*Pause.*)
> Nature!
> (*Pause.*)
> There's something dripping in my head.
> (*Pause.*)
> A heart, a heart in my head.
> (*Pause.*)

Thoughts of nature become reminders of mortality, and so oppressive that he imagines his heart dripping in his head.

Hamm's sense of his own degeneration stands in marked contrast to what has been called "the grain of time theme": the grains of time will never mount up to the impossible heap of infinity, but the heart's dripping does signify finite life; man is trapped in finite time. Hamm understands his helplessness, he knows he should end; yet still he seeks the means to stall. He is, for example, reluctant to finish his relationship with Clov —not for any love they share, but because Clov's leaving will be an ending, and Hamm hesitates at any ending. In their dialogue about the alarm clock, which will signal Clov's departure, Hamm grows tense, becoming first "angry" then "impatient" with Clov's banter. When the alarm rings through, Clov exclaims, "The end is terrific!" But Hamm, typically, "prefers the middle." After another exchange about the pain killer, Clov says his typical line: "I'll leave you." But this time the line bears more significance for Hamm. An ending has been not only discussed but planned; his next line is, "It's time for my story." Hamm uses this construction only once before, when he says, "It's time it ended," and he reiterates the themes of finishing and mortality before he begins the narrative. Thus Hamm implicitly pits his story against the prospect of ending life—his own life and life in the shelter. More than any of his other diversions, fiction releases him from the pains of tormented hesitation.

Hamm's story is successful not only as a diversionary tactic, but also as a balm for his mental and physical distress. Unlike the suffering Hamm of the present, his created "I" of the past is a self-styled Jehovah, regulating the weather (the earth then had a weather) with his instruments. Hamm agonizes over mortality, but his godlike protagonist ruthlessly denies life to a starving father and child on Christmas Eve. Unlike the hesitating Hamm, his fictional "I" is powerfully decisive. Through his story, Hamm achieves a completion, for by the end his protagonist has completed the action of denial: "He doesn't realize, all he knows is hunger, and cold, and death to crown it all. But you! You ought to know what the earth is like, nowadays. Oh I put him before his responsibilities!"

And yet Hamm's story fails to remove him from the tortures of the present. He terms his narrative a "chronicle," which is a record of events *in* time. If this is true, Hamm's protagonist is less a creation than a memory of the old Hamm; and we have only to look at the helpless figure slowly bleeding to death to realize that Hamm's "fiction," rather than releasing him from time, underscores the painful process of time. The story also fails because, as with everything else, Hamm is unable to finish it. The action of denial, so emphatic in the story, is undercut by a new development in the play. Clov claims that he sees a small boy outside the shelter, a "potential procreator." For Hamm, the boy is also a potential character for the chronicle, one who might revive the cycle of human suffering. His story ends on a note of resignation: "Well, there we are, there I am, that's enough."

The story itself, however, is an heroic achievement. Boxed within his shelter, surrounded by a "corpsed" world, Hamm recollects the past He knows that "soon there'll be no more speech," yet he speaks and creates. Fictionalizing is easier for Hamm than it will be for Winnie or the Mouth, but it is difficult nonetheless. Creating, like the other activities, is "slow work"; Hamm has to prod himself with "Well?" "And then?" in order to continue.

The situation in *Happy Days* intensifies the annihilation of *Endgame*. Hamm may be confined to a wheelchair, but Winnie is embedded in the earth—in Act I, up to her waist, in Act II, up to her neck. The inhabitants of the shelter play out their endgame under "grey light," while Winnie and Willie sit exposed under what Beckett calls "blazing

light'' (Winnie amends to ''hellish sun''). Winnie is caught in an interminable present so that words like ''day,'' ''daily,'' ''die,'' ''night''
signify nothing real but are merely vestiges of an ''old style.'' A shrill
piercing bell is the only marker in Winnie's day, the bell for waking and
the bell for sleeping.

In her timeless space, Winnie has her ''things,'' the contents of her
bag, which occupy her mind and occasionally expand her learning. After
repeated efforts, she deciphers the inscription on the toothbrush and
exclaims: ''That is what I find so wonderful, that not a day goes by—to
speak in the old style—hardly a day goes by without some addition to
one's knowledge.'' She also has her ''classics,'' though she has difficulty
remembering the lines of the passages. And she has Willie, a reluctant
conversationalist at best, but nevertheless one who listens.

> So that I may say at all times, even when you do not answer and perhaps hear
> nothing, Something of this is being heard, I am not merely talking to myself,
> that is in the wilderness, a thing I could never bear to do.

Hamm was able to bribe Nagg to listen to his story, but Winnie has to
be content with Willie's truculent responses. Yet he is the chief source of
her ''happy days.''

Despite her diversions, Winnie becomes increasingly aware of her
inability to act and effect action. Even in Act I, with the contents of her
bag still accessible, Winnie fears the ''evil hour'' when she wants to
perform an action (such as putting down the parasol) but is unable to do
so.

> Reason says, Put it down, Winnie, it is not helping you, put the thing down
> and get on with something else. (*Pause.*) I cannot. (*Pause.*) I cannot move.
> (*Pause.*) No, something must happen in the world, take place, some
> change.

Shortly after this speech the parasol bursts into flame. But no revelation
comes forth from this mock miracle. The parasol is back in Act II, while
Winnie has, inexplicably, sunk farther into the ground. In Act II, ''time''
is resurrected from the ''old style.'' Whereas Winnie in Act I could say,
''No better, no worse, no change,'' she is, in the second act, obviously
''worse'': ''To have been always what I am—and so changed from what I
was.'' Her cries to Willie become more urgent in Act II, but Willie will
not be roused into action.

To remove herself from the agonies of the present, and to counteract
her feelings of helplessness, Winnie composes stories. The Mr. and Mrs.

Shower or Cooker episode is not announced as a story; it "floats up" into her thoughts, as do her classics. They are perhaps a real couple who observe Winnie in passing, for in Act I, they see her as we see her, buried up to her waist. In Act II, however, the episode comes closer to being a fiction, because it removes Winnie from present time. One tormenting aspect of Winnie's situation is that in her days without end she cannot verify the past.

> I speak of temperate times and torrid times, they are empty words. . . . It is no hotter today than yesterday, it will be no hotter tomorrow than today, how could it, and so on back into the far past, forward into the far future. (*Pause*.) And should one day the earth cover my breasts, then I shall never have seen my breasts, no one ever seen my breasts.

Yet her breasts, not to mention her legs and shoulders are *discussed* by Mr. and Mrs. Shower ("Can't have been a bad bosom," he says, "seen worse shoulders in my day"). Winnie sees that they are no longer young ("Getting on . . . in life"); they in turn remember the past and ratify her existence in it. The couple not only look at her (Shower and Cooker derive from *schauen-kucken*, German for "look"), they react to her condition. Though Winnie cannot rouse Willie, Mr. Shower registers indignation at such inaction: "Why doesn't he dig her out?" he says.

Even more than the Shower-Cooker narrative, the Milly story in Act II releases Winnie from the present; through this fiction, she can conceive a temporal sequence: "A life. A long life. Beginning in the womb, where life used to begin, Mildred has memories, she will have memories, of the womb, before she dies, the mother's womb. She is now four or five already." Milly's dolly resembles both Winnie and Willie—*her* pearly necklet, *his* straw hat and blue eyes. Winnie and Willie are scarcely more lively than a waxen doll, but in creating the doll Winnie joins herself with Willie, thus fulfilling a desire through fiction. Most importantly, through the Milly story, Winnie can act and effect action. When the mouse runs up Milly's thigh, Winnie screams with her heroine, expressing for the first time her terror at Willie's protracted silence. Milly's screams bring the house down: "All came running . . . to see what was the matter . . . what on earth could possibly be the matter."

But the difference between fact and fiction is painfully obvious. No one "on earth" comes to Winnie's aid (Willie's intentions at the end are ambiguous). Like Hamm's chronicle, Winnie's stories reflect back on her real condition, which is a death in life. Her fictions are failures because they lure her away from the spirit of her "happy days": the Milly story ends with terror, and the Shower couple do nothing more than drag themselves "up and down this fornicating wilderness." Perhaps Winnie realizes this herself, for she closes the last narrative with, "Too late, too late."

Though her stories fail, Winnie's effort at fictionalizing are fully as heroic as Hamm's. Hamm's "we're getting on" sharpens to Winnie's "on"; with almost no dialogue to sustain her, she must energize herself, she must create something new under the blazing sun every time she opens her eyes.

Winnie, more than Hamm, draws our attention to the pains of creation. Her Milly story shows false starts, four times she refers to the failure or emptiness of words, and the "confused cries" in her head (reminiscent of the dripping in Hamm's head) reveal the extent of her own torment, despite her protestations of happiness. Winnie sees her last narratives through "the eye of the mind," a phrase which resonates beyond its reference to the imagination. Eyes, mouth, and mind are Winnie's last functioning parts. Amazingly enough, she is able to muster blinking, speaking, and thinking into creating fictions which remove her, however briefly, from the painful present.

From *Endgame* to *Happy Days* to *Not I*, Beckett moves his fictionalizers from a cell-like shelter to a mound of earth to a stage containing almost nothing. *Not I* lacks props, dialogue, and any semblance of surface reality. Humanity has shrunk to near anonymity. The nameless female speaker stands on a platform cloaked in darkness except for her dimly lit mouth; the nameless auditor, dressed in a black djellaba, is still except for four brief movements. *Not I* contains the longest of the three fictions. More accurately, *Not I* is *about* fictionalizing. The spoken content of the play consists entirely of the Mouth's fictional narrative. She attempts to remove herself from the experience of the present by objectifying that experience, by transmuting the time-bound "I" of autobiography into the "she" of fiction.

Unlike the stories by Winnie and Hamm, the Mouth's narrative moves back and forth in chronology. She begins at the beginning: "birth . . . into this world . . . this world . . . tiny little thing . . . before its time." The narration then jumps to the central scene. The woman, wandering in a field on an April morning, suddenly finds herself in darkness. She becomes almost "insentient," except for her hearing ("she could still hear the buzzing") and sight ("and a ray of light came and went"). She is unsure of her position, whether sitting, lying, kneeling, or standing. But the mind, she tells us, is still functioning: "but the brain still . . . still sufficiently . . . oh very much so! . . . at this stage . . . in control." That stage passes, however. Soon she hears herself speaking; a torrent of words comes rushing out, which her mind can neither grasp nor contain.

> imagine! . . . no idea what she's saying! . . . and can't stop . . . no stopping it . . . just as a moment before . . . a moment! . . . she couldn't make a sound . . . no sound of any kind . . . now can't stop . . . imagine! . . . can't stop the stream!

Then the narration moves back in time. Interwoven in the description of this April morning torrent are scenes from the past. We hear about the woman at a shopping center, unable to speak, simply passing in her list; we hear that she weeps, but only with effort recognizes her own tears; at court, again without speech, she merely waits to be led away. To these events must be added another: the time in April when darkness fell and the woman found herself speaking.

For the narration never progresses beyond that scene; like a cracked recording, it recapitulates the central scene again and again. The character is still caught in her April torrent, and it becomes clear that the Mouth's description of the outpouring is the outpouring we are hearing, as the darkness she describes is the darkness we see. The curtain falls on the Mouth melded with her fictional creation, questioning in the darkness, trying to "make sense of" her own torrent of words.

The Mouth's story does succeed in allowing "thoughts" to emerge. Like Winnie in the Shower Cooker story, the Mouth, from the posture of "oh long after" gains some perspective on existence. The darkness described at the beginning of the Mouth's narrative stimulates her "first thought," that perhaps she is being punished for her sins. Not because God is merciful (that notion occasions the only laughter in the play) but because darkness is generally considered terrifying. Then she realizes that she is not suffering—"indeed could not remember . . . offhand . . . when she had suffered less." So she dismisses the thought of punishment as "foolish." Yet she pursues the idea:

> unless of course she was . . . meant to be suffering . . . ha! . . . thought to be suffering . . . just as the odd time . . . in her life . . . when clearly intended to be having pleasure . . . she was in fact . . . having none.

The narrator perceives that there is no cause-and-effect relationship between the *feeling* of pain and pleasure and those experiences which we are told *produce* pain and pleasure. With this realization, she reintroduces the notion of punishment: being told that she should suffer when she might not be suffering *is* a punishment. However, she concludes this "first thought" with "vain reasonings."

And they are vain. The fiction fails because reason cannot order the clutter of experience. The thoughts that follow reveal a rapid disintegration; she makes no further attempt at analysis. With her second thought, she merely notes that feeling has returned to her body. Her third thought is a question; she wonders whether the torrent of words has any meaning. Her fourth thought is lost in the recapitulation of former motifs: her premature birth, the April morning before darkness fell. The mind struggles to objectify and reason, but the mind cannot work independently of memory and pain. Like Hamm's and Winnie's stories, the Mouth's fiction fails to remove her from present agonies. As with their fictions, her's underscores the confusion and torment of her condition.

Not I extends the problem of self in relation to fiction. The integrity of the mind is the last bastion of the self. In his lonely cell, on her desolate mound, Hamm and Winnie weave stories that respond to the needs of their innermost selves. In her darkness the Mouth also tries to weave, but in her case there is no distinction between the weaver and the web; in *Not I*, the mind will not mediate between words and experience. During the outpouring the mind "raves away on its own," producing memories, "dragging up up the past." Yet those memories are unrecognizable to the Mouth: she has "no idea what she is saying." For her the words have no referents; she is severed from the experience of her past life (memories), just as her mind is severed from the words which pour out of her mouth. But if the self makes no connection with the past or present, to what, then, does it connect? The fiction fails; we have seen that the "she" is no more than the fractured mirror of the "I." And it seems that the "I," too, is absent, for the mind of the "I" functions in neither present nor past. Perhaps the Mouth's self is that region, that "something" in the brain which begs the mouth to stop; this, however, is uncertain because the Mouth does not stop. Ultimately the "I," like the "she," is shrouded in darkness, and the self connects only to its last moving part: the Mouth.

Yet the Mouth speaks; and its attempt to fictionalize is as heroic as the efforts of Hamm and Winnie. More so: for words are not merely "old style," as in *Happy Days*, but they mean nothing to the Mouth. The hesitation and uncertainty which characterize the creative process in *Endgame* and *Happy Days* are present in every halting, incomplete phrase the Mouth utters. Twenty-one times the Mouth interrupts herself to ask "what?"—this compared to Hamm's small sprinkling of "Well?" and "And then?" Seven times the Mouth is reminded of the "buzzing" in her head, compared to Winnie's three references to the cries in her head. Toward this painful outpouring Beckett requests a particular attitude from his on-stage audience. At each mention (except for the last) of "what? . . . who? . . . no! . . . *she*" (not I), the silent auditor is to raise his arms from his sides and let them fall back "*in a gesture of helpless comparison.*" In all of Beckett's plays, there are no words as humane as this stage direction that follows the text of *Not I*. Against the silence of the stage, the silence of her life, the confusion in her own mind, the Mouth struggles. However failing, that struggle testifies to her heroism, and it invites our "helpless compassion."

The Mouth's fiction embraces and focuses the fictionalizing efforts in *Endgame* and *Happy Days*; her need to objectify experience is the impulse underlying the stories by Hamm and Winnie. Hamm's desire to finish, Winnie's desire to act, are rooted in the desire to be the objective controller rather than the subjective sufferer in life experience. For all three fictionalizers, present time is a process of inexorable degeneration. Hamm is finally fixed in his wheelchair; Winnie sinks further into the earth; and the human body is all but annihilated in *Not I*. For all three, the fictions are a salve to the pains of the present; the stories give the illusion of distance from the present. But they remain illusions. Like the Mouth's "she," Hamm's prating godlike "I" and Winnie's sheltered Milly are extensions of the time-bound self.

Being in the present, being in time is, finally, the only reality the self may know. And it is on this reality that the curtains close.

Dougald McMillan

Samuel Beckett and the Visual Arts: The Embarrassment of Allegory

Samuel Beckett is a man acutely aware of the visual arts and actively involved with them. One of his earliest fictional characters, Belacqua, is familiar enough with the National Gallery of Ireland to complain of how its paintings are displayed; he also knows the Dublin Municipal Gallery, formerly located in Charlemont House, and he is quite conscious of the architectural similiarities between Dublin's Pearse Street and Florence. After Beckett left Dublin, he remained close friends with the Irish painter, Jack Yeats—whose paintings he reviewed, admired, and hung in his apartment. Thomas McGreevy, the poet, art critic, and director of the National Gallery of Ireland, also remained a close contact in Dublin.

Beckett's travels during the *Wanderjahre* 1930–1937 seem often to have been dominated by his interest in art. To Lawrence Harvey he described his path through Germany in 1936 as "from museum to museum." The three notebooks of this trip are primarily records of paintings and music that impressed him. He recalls the kindness of Willi Grohmann, a director of the Zwinger Gallery, and he recalls the Nazi destruction of works of "decadent" art.

Some measure of the kind of artistic education Becket provided for himself in his wanderings can be gained through his allusions in the fiction. Through them his path can be traced to the National Gallery of England, the British Museum, the Louvre, the Prado, the Schatzkammer, Albertina, and the *Kunsthistorisches* Museum in Vienna, the Pinacoteca in Milan, the Uffizi and Santa Croce in Florence, the Sistine

Chapel in Rome, the Bishop's Palace in Würzburg, the *Stadtsgalerie* in Dresden, and the Campanella in Pisa—to name the most prominent. He also visited less well known collections or churches, such as those at Kassel, Chantilly, Hamburg, and Padua.

The breadth of his knowledge extends from ancient Chaldean to modern art. His essays and allusions indicate far more than a passing familiarity with schools of art ranging from the Norwich school of English landscape painting to the German post-expressionist movement. His knowledge encompasses a variety of genres ranging from traditional oil painting, sculpture, and engraving to surrealist collage and modern tapestry design. His concern for the visual extends to film, to fonts of type, and to figures that illustrate the principles of gestalt psychology.

Since settling in Paris, Beckett has been involved with the artists of the city. His *"La peinture des van Velde ou le monde et le pantalon,"* an exceptionally well-informed assessment of the situation of modern art criticism as well as modern painting, was evoked by an exhibition in 1945 at the Galérie Maeght. It was published in the influential *Cahiers d'Art.* His condensation of that article, *"Peintres de l'empêchement,"* appeared in the equally respected art journal *Derrière le Miroir.* His poem *"bon bon il est un pays,"* a comment on art as a self-contained world, was written at the request of Geer van Velde to accompany a painting in an exhibition. Not used for that occasion, it later accompanied an exhibition of the works of Avigdor Arikha, the Israeli artist and friend of Beckett. His *"Hommage à Jack B. Yeats"* was written as part of a symposium occasioned by Yeats's 1954 exhibition in Paris. Beckett also provided a short text in appreciation of the works of Henri Hayden for a 1952 exhibit. Even when he was forced by the Nazis to leave Paris and go into hiding in Roussillon, Beckett kept Jack Yeats's painting *Morning,* and it was partly his interest in art which helped establish his friendship with Henri Hayden during this period.

More recently Beckett has become involved in collaborative efforts with artists. Two of his most recent works are short texts selected especially to accompany original illustrations. In 1972 a section from *The Lost Ones* was chosen for illustration by Avigdor Arikha, who had previously illustrated *Stories and Texts for Nothing.* The result is a magnificent limited-folio edition entitled *The North.* Beckett provided an unpublished text, "Still" for another limited-folio edition illustrated with three engravings and three preliminary studies by the English engraver Stanley William Hayter. This edition was published by M'Arte Edizione of Milan in 1974. According to a newspaper account, Beckett has prepared a set of texts to accompany paintings by the American artist Jasper Johns for a book to be brought out by the Petersborough Press in 1975.

Beckett's most important critical statements have come in his essays on painting. In *"Le monde et le pantalon,"* *"Peintres de l'empêchement,"* and the "Three Dialogues" with Georges Duthuit, we find general observations on modes of criticism, on traditions of modern art, and on problems of the modern artist. In his essays on Denis Devlin and Rilke, the achievements and failures of Braque, Kandinsky, and Rodin define the position of the poet as well as that of the modern painter. And many critics have applied the dialogues with Duthuit to Beckett's own work.

Whether he is dealing with the visual arts or with literature, Beckett's concern is to define the changing relationship between the artist and the "occasion" of his art—the persistent need of the artist to express, even in the face of subject matter resistant to expression and an inadequate medium. In writing about the predicament of the modern artist faced with fundamental questions of representation, Beckett has implicitly defined his own position. He does not see himself in the narrow confines of a purely literary or theatrical tradition; rather he views himself in terms applicable to all artistic fields in this century. Beckett's criticism of art as well as of literature represents a significant body of commentary pertinent to his own work and that of his contemporaries—as much commentary as we have from Wallace Stevens or James Joyce, for example, and more than we have from many other modern writers.

Beckett's involvement with art is not merely the product of a superb education or a superficial interest. He seems personally preoccupied with art and the visual. If he reads about Descartes, he retains an awareness of the Hals portrait, which appears in "Whoroscope." He reads of the sigmoid "line of beauty" in Hogarth's *The Analysis of Beauty* and assimilates it to the curving line of the Dublin shoreline in "Serena III." He frequents Mt. Geneviève in Paris, and details of the church St. Étienne du Mont appear in "The Calmative." From the Sorbonne he retains the impression not of scholars but of the frescoes of Puvis de Chevannes, to which he alludes in "Sanies II." He lives in the 15th arrondissement, and the undistinguished municipal bust of M. Ducroix from the Rue Brancion appears in *The Unnamable*. He walks in Hyde Park, and *Murphy* is filled with accounts of not only Jacob Epstein's controversial sculpture *Rima* but also George Watt's *Physical Energy* and the statue of Queen Victoria. Murphy looks at the floor and sees in the linoleum pattern a resemblance to a Braque painting. Beckett discusses the problems of the modern writer with Tom Driver and makes his point by contrasting the Madeleine and Chartres cathedral. Where art is a part of his environment, Beckett perceives it consciously; where the environment suggests art, Beckett is aware of the connection.

Beckett's work, the fiction in particular, is pervaded by an aware-
ness of visual forms and techniques and allusions to works of art.
Beckett was quite conscious of this aspect of his work, sometimes found
it embarrassing, and struggled openly with it in the poems and novels.
Beckett's fiction reveals the most pervasive influence of the visual
arts. His Belacqua derives from Dante's description in canto IV of the
Purgatorio, which invites illustration. In the edition illustrated by Sandro
Botticelli, to whom Beckett refers several times in the early fiction and
poetry, Belacqua seated in a fetal position in the lea of his rock becomes an emblem of embryonic recoil from life and wearisome ascent.
Throughout his works Beckett presents his characters in this emblematic
posture and uses references to works of art to reinforce its suggestions.
Murphy, for example, who is so reluctant to leave his rocking chair and
his solipsistic interior world, "recruits himself" before the Harpy Tomb
in the British Museum, which depicts the dead as a seated figure enticed
by young girls to rejoin the living. Macmann on his park bench, aware
of but not part of the crowd he observes, is fixed by comparing his posture
to that of the seated statue of the Colossus of Memnon at Thebes.

The rich surface of references to works of art in *More Pricks than
Kicks* and the published parts of "A Dream of Fair to Middling
Women" is not just visual characterization. It is part of a conscious
aesthetic strategy. In "Echo's Bones," Beckett wrote of the old wound of
Belacqua's life that seemed never to heal. He had tried everything, we are
told, including fresh air, irony, and "great art." In the story "Yellow,"
Belacqua ransacks his mind for a suitable engine of destruction to deal
with painful thoughts. His solution is to admit them and then to "obliterate the bastards," "perforate his adversary" with laughter. He might also
have wept, "it came to the same thing in the end," but "weeping in this
charnel house would be misconstrued." In Beckett's early work, his
deliberate use of art is a tactic to place the painful experience depicted in
the poems of "Echo's Bones" in an ironic perspective and thus "obliterate" it. Even in "Echo's Bones" Belacqua's metamorphosis from a
realistic character in "Enueg I" to a comic caricature in "Malacoda" is
represented as part of a work of art. He is the *imago*, the butterfly, in a
floral painting by Jan van Huysum.

As the title suggests, *More Pricks* is the account of one who sets
out to oppose the world and ends up suffering from it. Through the
allusions to paintings, sculptures, and architectural forms, the protagonist Belacqua becomes a comic martyr—a veritable calendar of
sainthood and martyrdom: St. Paul, St. John, St. George, and St. Peter.
He sets out to "kick against the pricks" as did the Biblical St. Paul, but
he is more like the St. Paul of Rubens's *Conversion of St. Paul*, who,

blinded by God and menaced by the hooves of his own horse, can only throw up a hand to ward off further harm. As Belacqua says in "Yellow," he will return to the sanctuary of his own mind "before the world *kicks* him there" (emphasis added).

Belacqua thinks of himself as "an easy going St. George at the court of Mildendo" and even has a lady with a Pisanello face like that of the finely profiled Princess of Trebizond rescued by the lance-wielding St. George in Pisanello's painting in Verona. But in spite of Belacqua's determination to "perforate his adversary," his marriage to Lucy is a docile capitulation to domesticity which leaves him frustratedly throttling snapdragons in his garden at twilight. His second marriage, to Thelma bboggs of 55 North Great St. George Street, is a further capitulation. Neither Pisanello's St. George, nor Uccello's, nor any of the other lance-wielders is applicable, but rather Hogarth's etching, *The Court of Mildendo,* in which Gulliver is tied down and pricked with little darts to suffer a humiliating rectal infusion.

Belacqua's fate is summed up with a reference to Velasquez's *The Surrender of Breda,* which Beckett calls "The Lances." Like Pisanello's painting of St. George and Rubens's of St. Paul, the painting is centered on the great rump of a horse. On either side the lances of opposing armies are arranged in rows. In the center, one of the commanders hands a single key to the other. The reference underscores Belacqua's final defeat. "The body was between them on the bed like the keys between the nations in Velasquez's 'Lances,' like the water between Buda and Pest, and so on hyphen of reality." The lances are in the hands of the others: he is a passive victim. For Belacqua it is more pricks than kicks. Even in death he cannot escape. Smeraldina, who is called Belacqua's "spiritual equivalent," and Hairy, who gains new life from Belacqua's death, are living components of Belacqua, and their relationship will perpetuate the relationship of Smeraldina and Belacqua. He becomes the intermediary between them, the keys to the kingdom. "Peter, on this rock. . . ."

For Belacqua, whose life is a struggle to evade women, marriage is the principal martyrdom. As his bride approaches in "What a Misfortune," "Belacqua's heart made a hopeless dash against the wall of the box, the church suddenly cruciform cage, the bulldogs of heaven holding the chancel. . . ." "Ecce," hisses Hairy at this point. Again the whole visual tradition—Christian architecture and the *Ecce Homo*—is called into ironic juxtaposition with Belacqua's fate.

Compared to the psychological novels of Joyce and Proust, this art of displacement and obliteration makes these characters seem like "puppets." The many references to Rodin, Dürer, Epstein, Della Robbia, Velasquez, Tommaso, Uccello, and "the master of tired eyes," Paul Henry, and to annunciations and madonnas, serve to assure us that the author is aware of just how artificial his characters are. This technique is one of the most salient aspects of *More Pricks Than Kicks*. Belacqua in his characteristic posture is described in "A Wet Night" as "the central leaf on the main triptych his feet on a round so high that his knees topped the curb of the counter. . . ." He appears later in the story framed in a doorway in tableau. And lest we should miss it, the point is made quite explicitly in "Love and Lethe," where Ruby Tough is described as resembling "Magdeline[1] in the Perugino Pieta in the National Gallery in Dublin, always bearing in mind that the hair of our heroine is black and not ginger." The note expands the reference:

[1]The figure, owing to the glittering vitrine behind which the canvas cowers, can only be apprehended in sections. Patience, however, and a retentive memory have been known to elicit a total statement approximating to the intention of the painter.

In *Murphy* and *Watt* the visual arts become the vehicle for more serious commentary. The central issue of *Murphy*—the conflict between love and solipsism—is presented as a problem of visual perception in terms of figures of gestalt psychology, and its effects are presented by references to painting. "All life is figure and ground," says Neary at the beginning of the novel, "the face, or system of faces, against the big blooming buzzing confusion." His beloved Miss Dwyer is "the one closed figure in the waste without form and void!" But once attained, Miss Dwyer "became one with the ground against which she had figured so prettily." Neary's pursuit of the closed figure now centers on Murphy. For Neary the transformation of figure into ground is a loss. For Murphy it is at first a relief, "ground mercifully free of figure." Ultimately, however, the loss inherent in exclusion of others from perception becomes apparent to Murphy, too. Having seen himself as "a speck in Mr. Endon's unseen," Murphy himself is unable to evoke a mental picture of Celia or any other living creature. He sees instead only the confusion of partial images "evoking nothing . . . "reeled upward off a spool level with his throat." Murphy concludes that this reeling confusion "should be stopped, whenever possible, before the deeper coils were reached." The alternative to seeing "nothing" is "naught"—zero, the closed figure. The alternative to chaos is a perception of the face and a return to Celia. But Murphy does not embrace this alternative; he continues on into chaos. The only organized image in Murphy's mind is one depicting his sense of loss, pain, and terror: "the clenched fists and rigid upturned face of the child in a Giovanni Bellini Circumcision, waiting to feel the knife. He saw eyeballs being scraped first any eyeballs, then Mr. Endon's.'' The bulging terrified eyes of the children in Bellini's paintings, such as this one in the National Gallery of England, show the emotional effect of what has been presented in the more abstract terms of figure and ground. Irony is still present, but referring to the Bellini painting is a serious way of suggesting the terror that lies beneath the comic surface of the novel.

Beckett deals directly with paintings as allegorical expression in *Watt*. There he presents us with a series of pictures and openly invites us to contemplate their significance as commentary on the human predicament. Watt ''in search of rest, [thinks] of the possible relations between such series as these, the series of dogs, the series of men, the series of pictures. . . . ''

When we are first shown Watt's room, a color reproduction on his wall is referred to but not described. Attention is focused instead on the fine view from his window of the race course. Later, though, in the waiting room, a large colored print of the horse Joss emerges from the wall. It is a picture of a poor old horse, shown in the light of an impending storm or night, contemplating without appetite the sparse grass overrun with cockles. ''The horse seemed hardly able to stand. Let alone run.'' The allegory is clear enough. Picture one of the human condition, in Watt's view.

The second picture is the one that hangs in the upstairs room of Erskine, the servant with access to the master, Mr. Knott. It is of a black circle on a white background broken at its lowest point. Appearing to recede in the background is a blue dot. There is an illusion of movement in space and time and the possibility for the two forms to exist in the future or to have existed in the past on the same plane. Watt wonders what the artist intended to represent. Among the nearly limitless possibilities that can relate a center and a circle, one—''the thought that it was perhaps this, a circle and a center not its center in search of a center and its circle respectively, in boundless space, in endless time''—fills him with tears. Thus, the sense of incompleteness familiar in our visual experience extends to other parts of life as well.

The third picture is evoked when Watt is cut by the brambles and barbed wire fence that separates his garden from the narrator Sam's.

> His face was bloody his hands also and thorns were in his scalp. (His resemblance, at that moment, to the Christ believed by Bosch, then hanging in Trafalgar Square was so striking I remarked it.) And at the same

instant I suddenly felt I was standing before a great mirror in which my garden was reflected and my fence. . . .

The circular crown of thorns prominent in the Bosch *Scourging of Christ* in the National Gallery of England recalls the circular form of the race course seen from Watt's window, the unclosed circle of the painting in Erskine's room, and the echo of that pattern formed by the barbed wire fences as they bulge out to holes positioned opposite each other. The relationship of the series of pictures is first of all visual. They all present circularity. Through the painting by Bosch the implications of circularity in human existence are suggested.

The portrait in the Addenda presents an ironic allegory of the artist himself. The progression of Watt's perception of Joss had been from the general to the particular. "Watt identified, first the field, then the horse, and then thanks to an inscription of great   ?   , the horse Joss." The portrait of the artist in the Addenda is the last picture in the novel, and it is the most particular. The identity of the artist is the last detail to be discerned, and indeed it remains a question whether his identity is discernable at all.

Already in "A Casket of Pralinen for the Daughter of a Dissipated Mandarin," a poem published in *European Caravan* in 1932, Beckett reacted against stylized presentation of experience in terms of art. There he presented himself as Judas from a post-expressionist Last Supper and compared himself with Andrea Mantegna's *Cristo Morto* in the Pinacoteca in Milan, which he called a "butchery stout foreshortened Saviour." But at the center of the poem is a denial of this mode of presentation.

> Oh I am ashamed
> of all clumsy artistry
> I am ashamed of presuming
> to arrange words
> of everything but the ingenuous fibres
> that suffer honestly.

The parody of his own techniques in the portrait of the artist at the end of *Watt* reflects a similar sense of embarrassment at the disparity between direct presentation of "honest" suffering and dependence on allegory and art.

In the imaginary painting at the end of *Watt*, the artist is shown nude, seated at a piano with his genitals covered by a piece of stave paper. The idea of self-revelation is parodied by the combination of the nudity of the man, depicted in such naturalistic detail that muscles are described in anatomical terms and the dirt on his toenails is noticed, with the purely artificial and conventional sheet of music covering his genitals. The ludicrous attitude of the seated figure is an ironic treatment of the emblematic use of posture. One hand is on the piano, the other held to his ear to detect receding tones. His bare feet are one atop the other as in a crucifix. His expression is of a man "about to be delivered of particularly hard stool." (Cf. Belacqua's retreat to the toilet in "Sedendo et Quiesciendo" and, later, Lucky's dance in *Waiting for Godot*.)

The use of detail in allegorical fashion is also ridiculed. "The significant detail" of the painting, we are told, "would have done credit to Heem." Jan de Heem's *Fruit Piece with Skull, Crucifix, and Serpent* in the National Gallery of Ireland is typical of the combination of exacting fidelity to the natural object with symbolic meaning attached to the naturalistic details. (The catalog of the National Gallery even contains an explanation of the symbols in de Heem's work.)

The attempt to transfer the techniques of one artistic medium to another is a source of irony in the painting. The fictitious painter is referred to as "Black Velvet" O'Connery, recalling Jan "Velvet" Brueghel, who attempted to render all five senses visually in a series of allegorical paintings called *The Senses*. The attempt to achieve a cumulative effect of color is parodied by salient repetitions of "red," "red," "red." In a mockery of attempts to evoke auditory perception by visual means, Watt has no trouble identifying the chord in the painting as "C major in its second inversion." The prominence of the sheet of music is a comic representation of the centrality of music in a nonmusical medium. (Beckett had relied heavily on musical terminology in developing his aesthetic theories in "Dream," and music as transcendent experience had been important in "Echo's Bones" and *More Pricks than Kicks*.) The assimilation of sculpture to literary ends and the general confusion of one medium with another are made comic by Beckett's calling the figure in the painting a "bust" just after his breast has been described in detail.

But the most important question is whether the artist is revealed by the technique. He is not. Art Conn O'Connery, as the name implies, is a trick—a fictitious creation made up from bits and scraps of an artistic tradition. His connections with de Heem and Brueghel have been pointed out. His other components are to be found chiefly in the representations of the Irish school in the National Gallery of Ireland. The name is taken partly from James Arthur O'Connor, whose six oils make him one of the major representatives of the school. In part it comes from Rodrick

O'Connor, whose single painting, *Portrait of the Artist*, the gallery acquired in 1929. Probably (although it is uncertain how Beckett would have known of it since it was not acquired until 1951) the painting and the name owe something to Conn O'Donnell's *Portrait of Art O'Neill Harpist*, which depicts a blind harpist who is very nearly a caricature of the Homeric poet.

O'Connery is out of the "great Chinnery-Slattery tradition." The well-known Dublin artist George Chinnery had, like Beckett in "Dream," made a *Portrait of a Mandarin*, a large painting that dominates his section of the National Gallery. John Slattery's one painting in the Dublin museum is *Portrait of William Carelton Novelist*. The Addenda also associates O'Connery with "the master of the Leopardstown half-lengths." The Leopardstown racetrack, visible from the window of Beckett's birthplace in Foxrock, frequently provided subject matter for Beckett's friend Jack B. Yeats. Beckett shared with Yeats the tendency displayed in *Watt* to see in horses analogs to the human situation.

In the trilogy Beckett moves to rid the novels of the surrogates who suffer for him and the trappings of art that accompany them. Although it contains relatively few direct allusions to specific works of art, *Molloy* nevertheless reflects the influence of the visual arts. Molloy assures us that although he is "far from being an artist or an aesthete" he sees in a way "inordinately formal," and at another point he confesses to a "mania for symmetry." On their "unreal journey" he and Moran move about a circle divided into quadrangles, each associated with a stylized landscape of "plain," "mountain," "city," and "sea." The horizon is "burning with phosphorous and sulphur," and the sun is "a living tongue of flame darting toward the zenith." This grid of iconographic space owes more to the world of Gothic art than to real Ireland or the landscapes of literary allegory as in Spenser and Bunyan.

Over this grid are laid pastoral details that cause Moran to exclaim, "What a pastoral land," and to compare the concentration of perspective in one scene to that in a "painting by an old master." Molloy does not share Moran's enthusiasm for visual technique. "I apologize for all these details, in a moment we will go faster, much faster. And perhaps relapse again into a wealth of filthy circumstance. But which in its turn will give way to vast frescoes, dashed off with loathing. Homo mensura cannot do without staffage." Whatever embarrassment they may cause, these artificial details are an unavoidable part of the thought process producing the work. In *"Le monde et le pantalon"* Beckett had made a similar excuse for staffage as an unavoidable aspect of Claude Lorrain's painting.

The conflict between direct experience and artificial expression is also presented in the contrast between Molloy and Moran. Again Beckett depends upon allusions to art to undercut his dependence on it. Molloy, the primary actor whose homeward journey is undertaken alone and reluctantly as a result of compelling inner motivation, is depicted in the familiar posture of the Belacqua figure. Moran, the observer who leaves home so eagerly to execute the command to write a report on Molloy, tries the Belacqua posture briefly but rejects it. He prefers to imagine himself in the posture of Rodin's *Thinker* and his Ugolino from *Gates of Hell.* His attitude is undercut by making the popular statue into a joke. Moran sits atop a milestone "eyes fixed on the earth as on a chess board . . . coldly hatching plans for the next day for the day after, creating time to come."

Moran's facile attachment to the world is further ridiculed by a reference to Rodin's sculpture *The Burgesses of Calais,* in which six downtrodden citizens, linked together by a bronze rope trudge in a weary circle. Moran would like to bind his son to him with a rope but fears that his son might untie himself and he would be left trailing one end behind him "like a burgess of Calais." This image of one of the burgesses detached from the others, trailing his bronze rope behind him, is preposterous. Like Rodin, whom Beckett had disparaged in "Smeraldina's Billet Doux" and his review of Rilke's *Poems,* Moran is too eager to insert himself in allegory, while masquerading as a realist. Significantly, Moran is going to force his son to learn double-entry bookkeeping. In his review of Jack Yeat's *Amaranthers,* Beckett had derided allegory as "that glorious double entry, with every credit in the said column, a debit in the meant." Molloy at least is aware that he is imposing staffage on others, and he apologizes for it, promising relief in the future. Moran shows no such consideration.

The embarrassment of "clumsy artistry" reaches a climax in *Malone Dies,* where Malone speaks of his heart "burning, with shame, of itself, of me, of them of everything except beating apparently." "Don't fret about our methods," the narrator says, "leave that to me." The narrator's attempt to "empty out" from his head in a "gurgle of outflow" all the characters that have peopled the previous fiction coincides with his attempt to divest himself of a dependence on visual art as a means of representing the world. This is his "last journey down the long familiar galleries." (Molloy had referred to his characters as a "gallery of moribunds.")

As the inmates of St. John of God's are about to be dispatched by Lemuel, the narrator declares, "The window, I shall not see it again."

He has come to associate this window with a world of artificial perception which is being superseded and rejected. Early in the novel the pane has revealed a night like those depicted in the works of Kasper David Friedrich. The pane is frosted, and Malone wishes he could breathe on it. Later the window is compared to the *trompe l'oeil* window complete with painted stars by Giovanni Tiepolo in the Bishop's Palace in Würzburg. But finally, artistic presentation no longer is sufficient: Malone must assure himself that what he sees is real. "The black night I see is truly of mankind and not merely painted on the window pane, for [the stars] tremble like true stars, as they would not do if they were painted."

Violets, roses, and cupids that formerly decorated the ceiling of Malone's chamber hang down in fragments or have disappeared, but a sense of baroque extravagance remains in the window and in the white, blue, pink, and gold figures revealed in it. In the room, as in the Bishop's Palace, where Tiepolo's frescoes of each continent cover the ceiling, all heaven and earth have, through the tricks of painting, been brought into the interior so that the human body exists in an absurd scale. Malone's feet are "leagues away," his hands are "in other latitudes," his stick is at "one of the poles" or "the equator," his feces might fall in Australia. If he stood up he would fill "a considerable part of the universe."

Malone—swollen, discolored, with feet thrust forward in distorted perspective, on his deathbed on "Easter week-end spent by Christ in hell"—is like the realistic *Cristo Morto* already identified with disingenuous artistry in "A Casket of Pralinen." He is an incongruous figure to be found among Tiepolo's allegorical baroque frescoes. The absurdity of Mantegna's morbid Christ in Tiepolo's exuberant world is, itself, ironic commentary on the disparate union of art and experience in the fiction.

Malone would like to leave this world. "One last glimpse and I feel I could slip away as happy as if I were embarking for—I nearly said Cythera, decidedly it is time for this to stop. After all this window is whatever I want it to be. . . ." Even as he announces his desire to leave, another parallel from painting crowds into his expression. In leaving, he would be like one of the figures in Watteau's *Embarkation for Cythera* in the Louvre, where a party of voyagers spirals out of a nineteenth-century landscape toward an indistinct destination in the far distance. The members of the procession change from real people in the foreground to undetermined cherublike forms in the distance. The scene is reminiscent of Saposcat's attempt to "glide away" out of a world of pastoral staffage and carefully arranged visual perspectives. Malone seems unable to avoid allusions to art. He is an old tourist and, like

Murphy, "one of the elect who require everything to remind them of something else." But he is impatient with this tendency and is determined to make an end of it.

Therefore photographs begin to replace paintings as the main mode of self-presentation. Although we are told of photographs of the narrator and Macmann's beloved, Moll, the transition from the images of art to those of reality is not complete. "My photograph," says the narrator, but it is a picture of an ass in a bowler. It is only a middle stage between allegory and direct representation. Furthermore, the figure is blurred by the "operator's giggle." "Clumsy artistry" still remains. The picture of Moll at age fourteen seems more authentic, but Macmann tears it up and scatters it to the winds.

Art and allegory remain in the novel in Moll's carved ivory earrings representing the "two thieves" and the carved tooth showing the crucifixion. And, most of all, they remain in Macmann, Malone's creation. He may be found in the heart of the city near a real hotel, but he takes his form from the Colossus of Memnon, whose "planes" and "angles" define his emblematic posture. However, the process of disentanglement from art is ostensibly complete at the end of *Malone Dies*.

The Unnamable will talk of himself directly, abandoning all the characters enlisted formerly. He is also "done with windows" and "old pictures." In his curious position as observer at the center of a circle, viewing objects that pass before him at regular intervals, he contrasts the real with the conventions of art. A face might pass by: "A face . . . demonstrating all a true face can do . . . worth ten of St. Anthony's pig's arse." His own identity is readily available from a true photograph. "This is you. Look at this photograph. . . . I assure you . . . look at this photograph you'll see."

Whatever doubts remain, the question of identity no longer is obscured by art. Unlike the paintings, which obliterate and conceal experience, the photograph reveals it, and yet the process of revelation is not so final as it seems. The Unnamable does "invent another fairy tale"; he reverts to fables of Mahood and Worm. And just as he feels he is about to be grasped, he says, "Can it be they are resolved at last to seize me by the horns? Looks like it. In that case tableau any minute." The tableau of the novel is Mahood's world in the Rue Brancion, where across from the slaughterhouse for horses, he is fixed in a pot under the gaze of M. Ducroix, "the apostle of horsemeat." The Rue Brancion, the bust, and the slaughterhouse exist, but this is another stylized presentation resembling a work of art.

Even the Unnamable, who is so eager to express himself directly, has not stopped thinking of himself in terms of art. "I am Matthew and I am the angel," he says, envisioning himself as part of a scene from an unidentified painting, which is described in *Murphy* as "Luke's portrait with the angel perched like a parrot on his shoulder." This is his image of interior self-perception. He is both the poet and the paraclete-like being that speaks to him.

And while the Unnamable may prefer a real face to one of St. Anthony's visions, the mention of St. Anthony in connection with his world is enough to recall Hieronymus Bosch's nightmarish paintings of those visions. The Unnamable's world seems analogous to Bosch's *Garden of Earthly Delights* in the Prado. The Unnamable appears to realize the similarities between the world and Bosch's triptych with panels of Eden, the Earth, and Hell when he says, "I am forgetting the fires, unusual hell when you come to think of it, perhaps it's paradise, perhaps it's the earth, perhaps it's the shores of a lake beneath the earth." Whether or not this is intentional allusion, the details of the Unnamable's great desert on the shores of a lake filled with talking spheres, "crystalline impotences," great perforated egg-shaped beings, disembodied ears, and bodies writhing in torment bear striking resemblance to the details of Bosch's painting. The vestiges of art persist as part of the mental landscape of the trilogy.

Direct presentation of ingenuous suffering is partly achieved in *How It Is*, in those portions that purport to be memories of the narrator's "life above." "This is my life," he insists. "No stories but mine. No more figures." Experience is depicted without the use of art forms, not even photographs. When a scene of the narrator as a young child praying at his mother's knee is presented, we are not told that it is based on an actual photograph of Beckett and his mother. Instead of needing to apologize for the presence of art, the narrator seems briefly to feel himself too exposed without it. Thinking of how he will be revealed as the parts of his story unfold, he says, "Thalia, for pity's sake a leaf of thine ivy." The old theatrical masks are gone, and he feels their absence.

The portions of *How It Is* which deal with the journey through the mud are still dominated by the influence of the visual arts. The seemingly gratuitous turnings face down, face up, half-side left, half-side right; the carefully described patterns of chevrons and deasils; the dance-like movement "dextrogyre and sinestro"; and the detailed configurations of arms are not arbitrary or unprecedented. Like the movements of the angels in Blake's frontispiece to the Book of Job, the turns and spirals of Beckett's figures into and out of the world of experience are significant movements. (In this connection it should be noted that Beckett makes specific allusions to Blake's etchings for the Book of Job in *Murphy*.) The configurations of the arms recall Botticelli's illustrations to *Paradiso* from the same edition in which his Belacqua appears. There the changing angles of the arms of Beatrice and Dante indicate the degree of their progress.

In *How It Is* Beckett found the means to present experience directly and still to retain the emblematic mode that had been so important for him since the creation of Belacqua. In the fiction since *How It Is,* Beckett continues to employ this kind of emblematic statement that associates his work with the visual arts. The suitability of these works for illustration reflects the role the visual arts played in their origin: The posture of the crouched figures in *Imagination Dead Imagine* is itself a statement of their predicament. The similar figure from *The Lost Ones* is a visual condensation so graphic that the section could be extracted without being destroyed, and it was printed separately as *The North,* accompanied by Avigdor Arikha's sensitive etching of the figure. We might say of Arikha's etching, which echoes the lines of Botticelli's Belacqua, that it is out of Botticelli by Beckett.

In "Still" we can see how durable the images of art are for Beckett. The seated figures of Belacqua, Murphy, and Macmann are defunct, but still their essence remains in the description of a man seated in his room. The title suggests both the quietude of the man and the persistence of the figure. "Legs side by side broken right angles at the knees as in that old statue some old god twanged at sunrise and again at sunset." Here we can recognize not only the form of Macmann but also the statue of Memnon at Thebes moved to life at sunrise and sunset. This is not lifeless art—art unmoved by experience. There is "some reason some time past this hour" why the man should be moved by the sunset. But in the process of distillation over time, it is not the experience itself, but the response embodied in forms of art, which remains.

In the margin of the facsimile of the manuscript provided in the M'Arte edition are Beckett's own drawings. They reveal his preoccupation with the visual forms in which his characters are embodied. In one of them, strong black lines perpendicular to each other trace a broad W set on its side so that its lines are perfectly vertical and horizontal—the outline of a straight-backed chair. The body that fits this form is represented by a stylized sigmoid line sketched in lighter lines. The head is a series of scribbled circles in the same lighter line. Here, once again, it is the basic sense of visual form and not the details of naturalistic presentation which prevail. From the earliest stories to "Still," this strong sense of the visual derived from art pervades Beckett's works. His fiction is partly the record of his struggle to accommodate the forms and techniques of art to the necessity of "honest" expression. The willingness to display the struggle is itself a form of honesty which Beckett has admired in contemporary visual artists and which places him in their tradition.

Selected Bibliography of Books in English

Abbott, H. Porter. *The Fiction of Samuel Beckett* (Berkeley, Calif., 1973).

Blau, Herbert. *The Impossible Theatre* (New York, 1964).

Chevigny, Bell Gale. *Twentieth Century Interpretations of "Endgame"* (Englewood Cliffs, N.J., 1969).

Coe, Richard. *Samuel Beckett* (New York, 1964).

Cohn, Ruby. *Back to Beckett* (Princeton, 1973).

————, ed. *Modern Drama*, Beckett issue, (December, 1966).

————, ed. *Casebook on "Waiting for Godot"* (New York, 1967).

————. *Samuel Beckett: The Comic Gamut* (New Brunswick, 1962).

Duckworth, Colin. *Angels of Darkness* (London, 1972).

Esslin, Martin, ed. *Samuel Beckett* (Englewood Cliffs, N.J., 1969).

————. *The Theater of the Absurd* (New York, 1968).

Federman, Raymond. *Journey to Chaos* (Berkeley, 1965).

———— and John Fletcher, *Samuel Beckett: His Works and His Critics* (Berkeley, 1970).

Fletcher, John. *Samuel Beckett's Art* (New York, 1967).

———— and John Spurling. *Beckett: A Study of His Plays* (New York, 1972).

Harrison, Robert. *Samuel Beckett's "Murphy"* (Athens, Ga., 1968).

Harvey, Lawrence. *Samuel Beckett: Poet and Critic* (Princeton, N.J., 1970).

Hassan, Ihab. *The Literature of Silence* (New York, 1967).

Hayman, David, ed. *James Joyce Quarterly,* Beckett issue, (Summer, 1971).

Hesla, David. *The Shape of Chaos* (Minneapolis, Minn., 1971).

Kenner, Hugh. *A Reader's Guide to Samuel Beckett* (New York, 1973).
―――. *Samuel Beckett* (Berkeley, Calif., 1968).
―――. *The Stoic Comedians* (London, 1964).
Kern, Edith. *Existential Thought and Fictional Technique: Kierkegaard, Sartre, Beckett* (New Haven, Conn., 1970).
Knowlson, James, ed. *Samuel Beckett: An Exhibition* (London, 1971).
MacWhinnie, Donald. *The Art of Radio* (London, 1959).
O'Hara, John, ed. *Twentieth Century Interpretations of "Molloy," "Malone Dies," "The Unnamable"* (Englewood Cliffs, N.J., 1970).
Reid, Alec. *All I Can Manage, More Than I Could* (Dublin, 1968).
Robinson, Michael. *The Long Sonata of the Dead* (New York, 1969).
Scott, Nathan A. *Samuel Beckett* (New York, 1965).

Catalog

If you are interested in a list of fine Paperback
books, covering a wide range of subjects
and interests, send your name and address,
requesting your free catalog, to:

McGraw-Hill Paperbacks
1221 Avenue of Americas
New York, N.Y. 10020